Writing For I

A Collection of Works by

M.J. Fahy, Lyn Flanders, Yvonne Marjot, Ian Stewart and Karen Taylor

Writing For Rescue

Copyright 2014

Introduction.

The contributors to this book have come together through one common interest, animal rescue and protection. The proceeds of this book will go to a Romanian rescue centre, established to alleviate the suffering of the abandoned animals there and to give them a sanctuary from the appalling abuses they suffer from the Romanian officials and public shelters established there. Many animals are adopted to other countries in a bid to save them, but many more languish behind in horrific conditions that are traumatic to even consider, let alone live in.

To everyone that has bought this book – thank you. You have helped save countless lives and contributed directly to the spaying and neutering necessary to help alleviate the suffering.

Norah's Ark

By

Yvonne Marjot

http://www.amazon.co.uk/Yvonne-Marjot

Yvonne Marjot was born in England, grew up in New Zealand, and now lives on an island off the West Coast of Scotland. She has a Masters in Botany from Victoria University of Wellington, and a keen interest in the interface between the natural and human worlds. Her first novel, 'The Calgary Chessman', was published in 2014 by Crooked Cat Publishing, Edinburgh.

She has always made up stories and poems, and once won a case of port in a poetry competition (New Zealand Listener, May 1996). In 2012 she won the Britwriters Award for poetry, and her first volume of poetry, 'The Knitted Curiosity Cabinet', was published in 2014 by Indigo Dreams Publishing.

"Come on, kids, the water's nearly up to the doorstep."

Norah balanced the twins on either hip as she wedged one foot, and then the other into her Wellingtons. She wobbled as Japh made a grab for her earring, then stepped off into the water sloshing past her front doorstep. Fortunately the 4-by-4 sat high on its massive tires, well above the water level in the road. At the rate the flood was rising, though, it wouldn't be long before it was too dangerous to leave.

Sulie pushed past her and wriggled into the middle spot between the two car seats. She deftly buckled herself in and helped Norah to secure the twins. Jemmy squeaked as his harness clicked shut, then giggled as Sulie tickled his tummy. Norah could feel the pressure of the water flowing down the road. It pushed against the back of her boots. She looked round to see if other neighbours were also leaving, but all the doors down the street were tight shut. Perhaps they'd all left already.

She took a quick head count. In the back of the vehicle Spot and Merry whined in unison, and she could hear the guinea pigs scratching in their travel basket. The lorikeets' cage was safely stowed on the floor in front of the passenger seat, with plenty of room for Sam's legs.

Sam. Where was he? A frown creased her face as she worked her way through her worry list. Food – check. Spare clothes – check. Pet supplies – check. Dogs – guineas – rat…

Rats. That's where Sam would be. She plunged back into the house, not bothering to remove her wellies. Give it an hour and the water would be through the whole lower storey anyway. This weather! She hadn't seen anything like it in all the years they'd lived in Shottom-by-the-River. For the first time she realised what 'by-the-River' could actually mean.

Sam was upstairs, trying to secure the door of the rats' cage. Pinky and Poppy were huddled together in a pile of straw, staring at him. It was as if they understood what was coming. Norah brushed the hair out of her face wearily before she spoke to him, trying to keep exasperation out of her voice.

"Sam, I thought we were going to leave the rats? There's no room in the car. With plenty of food and water they can easily last a week."
"No, I can't leave them to drown."

"Oh, honey, the water's not going to come up this far."

She injected a note of jolly confidence into her words, but to be honest her heart was with Sam on this one. Who knew what tomorrow might bring, or how high the waters might rise? He looked up at her, white-faced, one hand stubbornly wrapped around the handle of the cage.

"Come on, then. I'll bring the cage and you carry their blanket."

Sam stood on the doorstep as Norah waded to the car and deposited the rats on the driver's seat. Then she carried Sam to the passenger side and decanted him carefully into the seat. "You're a weight, my boy," she said, hiding her fears under a joke, as she so often did. "Get yourself strapped in and then I'll give you the rats to hold." Carefully she made her way back to the driver's side. The water was already above the tops of her boots, and they had filled with water, the weight of them dragging at her as she walked.

She cast one look back at her front door. There seemed no point in closing it; the water was already lapping at the sill. She perched on the edge of her seat and pulled off her wellies. She tipped them upside-down, adding their contents to the ever-increasing volume of water sweeping down the lane. She shoved them under the seat, along with her soaked socks, and applied her bare feet to the pedals. As she snapped her seatbelt shut she made one final check - that Sam's belt was done up, and the three in the back seat were ready to go. Sam draped the blanket over the cage on his lap and the silent agitation of the rats calmed.

Norah resisted the urge to watch her house in the rear-view mirror as they drove slowly along the lane. It was only a house. All the important things were right here with her in the car – all but one. The 4-wheel-drive vehicle made short work of the two feet of water in the lane, and surged forwards as they gained the higher ground at the far end of the village. Ahead, perched on the top of the hill, she could see their destination.

"The Ark and Courage" had been a pub from time immemorial. No-one knew how it had come by its peculiar name. It was familiar ground to Norah, because before the kids were born she'd been the barmaid there, and then the proprietor's wife. Now she came to him, bringing all the things that he cared most about in the world. 'My wife, my kids, my animals. That's what matters. Anything else is just window-dressing. You're what matters to me."

For the first time that day, Norah began to feel calm. She'd done what she needed to do, and now she wouldn't have to cope on her own any more. If anyone knew what to do in this situation, Philip Noah would know.

He was there in the doorway as she pulled into the pub car park, striding forward to help Sam with the rats. Norah climbed out and went to open the back doors, but was delayed briefly by his hand on her arm and the warmth of his kiss. She smiled in relief at his kind, wonderful, utterly reliable face. "There you are, Mrs Noah," he said. "What about this British summer, eh?"

Midnight

By

M.J. Fahy

http://www.amazon.co.uk/M.J.-Fahy

for Sally, Nipper, Ronald and Reggie; dear little Rodney, Tufty; the two Sooties; Stumpy
Scrappy, Jeff, Norman, Gerby, Honey, Spotty, Choochy, and the two feathered Freddies.

,

M.J. Fahy lives on the south coast of England with her husband, two adult children, two dogs, a deaf cat, and two elderly hens. She writes Middle Grade children's stories in a cosy shed in her garden (which her husband built), though quite a lot of time there is spent daydreaming, mostly about magical places, people, and animals.

As a child she begged and nagged her parents for a dog or cat for years, to no avail, until her thirteenth birthday when she was taken to a house and allowed to choose a puppy. Of course she chose the smallest hiccupping pup of the litter; this was Nipper, a Cocker Spaniel cross; her friend and confidante for another thirteen years.

She chose to write a children's story for this book, about an animal-loving child's profound yearning for their very own pet, something she remembers with clarity.

On his tenth birthday, Trevor receives a special pet from an eccentric neighbour. The animal is Midnight, a cat that can transform into many other animal forms and also helps Trevor at school with his maths. He has to keep Midnight hidden, but unfortunately, Trevor's mother eventually finds out about the cat and insists he takes it back to the oddball neighbour, with surprising consequences.

CHAPTER ONE

Desdemona

'If I've told you once, I've told you a thousand times – you are *not* having a *pet!*'

'But the other day you asked me what I wanted for my birthday,' said nine year-old, soon to be ten year-old, Trevor Talbot. 'It doesn't have to be a dog or cat, though that'd be nice … A budgie would do.' He stared imploringly at his mother, who ironed one of his T-shirts so hard it looked like she was trying to press it right through the ironing board.

Mrs Talbot stopped and closed her eyes, then rubbed her forehead. 'I'm not having some mangy animal shedding fur all over my sofas. And as for birds–' She harrumphed loudly at this suggestion; 'No, no, no. One word, Trevor: *Seed!* It'll get dropped everywhere and it'll
be me hoovering every day. So, no pets – end of discussion!'

'Takes two people to have a discussion,' muttered Trevor.

'What's that?'

'Nothing.'

Trevor wasn't a sulker. He simply finished his breakfast, put his dish in the sink, and went out of the kitchen. He struggled down the hallway pretending to walk through deep snow and then climbed the stairs like he was scaling a mountain, on his tummy, stretching up with one probing hand at a time. It took him a full ten minutes to get to the top. On reaching the landing he turned and looked down at the precipice he'd traversed. *Not bad.* It was much steeper than the mountain he'd climbed the day before. *Tomorrow I'll have a go at Mount Everest,* he thought, *that'll take ages.*

Brushing his teeth in the bathroom a few minutes later, Trevor faced the mirror. Pale skin, a million freckles and red hair so thick that it had a life of its own was reflected back at him. He rinsed his toothbrush and wiped his mouth on a towel, leaving a white toothpastey smear. It was a shame, he thought, not being allowed a pet. A pet would have kept him company. Lots of other kids had brothers and sisters to play with when the weather was too bad to go out. What did he have? He sighed. *Never mind, I can always go to Joe's house and ask if I can take his dog up the park.*

Joe Moles was a neighbour who could be a bit quiet and grumpy, but who occasionally let Trevor take his elderly Golden Labrador out on walks. Although, Dreadnought wasn't that much fun as a playmate if he was being honest. Sometimes, usually after a few minutes, Trevor would find himself dragging the dog along the pavement as Dreadnought fought to go home to his comfy basket. Then the dog would grumble and growl at other dogs in the park, so that his arm would almost be pulled from the socket when Dreadnought strained on the lead. Trevor always went home with arm ache. He thought Joe's grumpiness had definitely rubbed off on his dog.

Definitely.

He did rather like Joe's old mother though. She smelled a bit like spices and herbs and cat wee, but she was funny and made Trevor the most delicious hot chocolate. Her name was Desdemona and at the last count she had nineteen cats of all colours and ages. Trevor's mum didn't like him calling on Joe and Desdemona Moles, because she said his clothes smelled funny after. So he kept his visits secret and when he went home he sprayed himself with plenty of fabric freshener.

Failing that, he had his books.

Trevor loved reading, which was why he enjoyed so many story-book adventures of his own. One day he could be scaling a mountain, the next, trying to cut the heads off a gazillion-headed Hydra. Or he could be shipwrecked on a rug-shaped island where the only provisions to be found for the whole day was a half-empty bottle of flavoured water and a whitish, powdery Easter egg he'd forgotten about, which he'd found under his bed after six months. Once, he'd had to rescue a princess (really his moth-eaten teddy bear, Ted) from an ogre, but it had ended badly when the princess had thrown up over him when he'd gone to kiss her (well, it had really been *him* who'd thrown up – on account of eating a mouldy Easter egg the day before). He'd lost a good companion because of that stupid egg: his mum had put poor sick-covered Ted into the washing machine, whereupon the elderly plush toy had promptly fallen to bits. Trevor had slid Ted's parts into a cereal box and buried him in the garden. Stories ended like that sometimes, they couldn't all have happy endings.

Still staring in the mirror, Trevor crossed his fingers and made a spur-of-the-moment wish, even though wishes never came true (it was a well-known fact). *For my birthday tomorrow I wish I could have a pet, please. It can be any animal at all. Nothing specific. Just any old animal will do. Thank you very much.*

Going to his room, Trevor quickly dressed and brushed his hair, which continued to still stick out in all directions. Then he went to his bookcase and chose a book to read before bed. He placed the dinosaur book on his pillow. Next, he went to the window and looked out at the little cul-de-sac of old houses. Forsythia Close was a nice place to live, if a little quiet. Trevor's parents were divorcing, so he and his mum had moved to the edge of the small town from the city a year ago to start again. He didn't see his dad very often, though a card would probably arrive with some money in for his birthday, so his mum said.

Early Saturday mornings could be a good starting point to an adventure, thought Trevor, especially after making a wish. He decided there and then that he *would* call on Joe Moles. You never knew what could happen in a massive park. He and Dreadnought might find a wormhole to another dimension hidden behind a bush or something? Dogs were always finding random stuff. Then if the wormhole took them to another time, or planet even, Dreadnought would have to have a bit more *Oomph* about him to survive, wouldn't he?

So Trevor thundered down the stairs and went to the door.

'Where're you off to?' called his mum from the kitchen.

'Um, just out to play. Park, I expect.'

'All right. No talking to strangers, though. And be back for lunch.'

'Okay. See you.'

It took exactly thirty-one steps to bring Trevor to the Moles' front door. He rang the bell. No one answered. He rang again, and waited. From what sounded like far away came a faint shuffling; then there was a rattling and scraping. The security chain stopped the door from opening fully. A brown, wrinkled, face with black sparkly eyes peered through the gap.

'Aha, it's only you, Trevor. Come to see Dreadnought, have you?'

'Yes, please, Desdemona, if that's all right?' Trevor was allowed to call Mrs Moles by her first name – the elderly woman insisted on it.

The chain was detached and the door opened wide. 'Come away in, child. There's been a bit of sad news. I'll tell you all about it over some cocoa.'

*

'Poor Dreadnought,' said Trevor, wiping his eyes with a sleeve.

'I know,' said Desdemona, sadly, stroking a large white cat sitting on her lap. 'Joe phoned me from the vet's. He's absolutely distraught. Carried him the whole way, he did. But at least Dreadnought didn't suffer. He passed away before Joe got him there. A stroke, most likely, so the vet says.'

'Oh,' said Trevor, not really knowing what a stroke was and thinking that he'd better look it up in his dictionary went he got home.

'Drink your chocolate up,' said Desdemona, peering over the top of her purple-tinted spectacles, which always perched precariously on the tip of her nose. 'Something sweet to drink is like medicine when you've had a shock.'

Trevor nodded and took a gulp of the rich velvety liquid, which seemed a bit different than usual. 'Tastes funny,' he mumbled into the mug.

'Does it now, young man?' Desdemona laughed, displaying a row of gleaming gold teeth. Placing the white cat on the floor, she got up from her chair at the kitchen table and shuffled over to an old dresser – where row upon row of bottles and jars were kept – and, brushing several cats out of the way, pointed to a small blue bottle. 'That's probably 'cause I added a few drops of what I call *Banish Birthday Blues!* So you'd best drink till that mug's empty – only way it'll work.'

Trevor did as he was told, and drank, even though he couldn't remember telling Desdemona that it was his birthday tomorrow? But he must've let it slip out sometime, mustn't he?

He watched the old woman take his mug and wash it in the sink. For the year he'd known Desdemona, she'd always worn the same electric-blue, satiny dress (though maybe robe with baggy sleeves would describe it better), with lots of bead necklaces hanging around her neck. And every day she had some kind of bright flower pushed into her white fluffy-cloud hair, even in wintertime. She was as dazzling as the kitchen, thought Trevor, wishing his mum would paint their walls in something other than beige.

Just then, Trevor heard the sound of the front door opening and closing. He gulped. What would he say to Joe, whose only friend had seemed to be his dog?

The tall man stood in the kitchen doorway. 'Trevor,' said Joe, by way of greeting.

Trevor stared at Joe's drawn face and bloodshot eyes.

'Hello, Joe … So sorry about your sad loss.' Trevor had seen his mother write that in a card to one of her distant relatives once. He thought it might do.

'Cheers.'

Trevor studied the patterned tablecloth as Joe went over to his mother and gave her a swift hug. Then Desdemona reached up and stroked her middle-aged son's cheek.

In silence, Joe left the kitchen and went upstairs.

'Going to be hard,' Desdemona said, sighing. 'That dog was everything to him. He would've been totally housebound if it wasn't for Dreadnought. Never has liked mixing, that boy … always craved solitude. Doctors never could find …' Desdemona cleared her throat. 'Anyway, less of the doldrums, what do you say about a few games of Old Maid?'

'Yes, please,' said Trevor, nudging a ginger cat out of the way to clear a space on the table.

They played for the rest of the morning until it was time for him to go home for lunch. In truth, Trevor would've rather stayed. Old Maid and cats were a brilliant combination to while away the time, but his mum would worry. He was only nine till tomorrow. When he was ten it'd be different; he'd be old enough to go to loads of different places on his own and stay out a lot longer, almost till dark. *You can do that when you're ten.*

Desdemona wiped the chocolate moustache from his face with an odd-smelling damp cloth then walked him slowly to the front door. She gave him a hug. He held his breath when his face pressed into her electric-blue satiny-ness.

'Bye – bye, Trevor. Have a lovely birthday tomorrow.'

'Thanks, Desdemona.'

When he reached the front gate, the old woman suddenly called out to him: 'And I'd check the garden shed first thing in the morning, too. You might find something of interest in there.'

Puzzled, he just nodded, smiled and waved and then went home to spray his clothes.

CHAPTER TWO

The Gift

The following day was a blur of activity, beginning with Mrs Talbot handing Trevor an envelope from his dad. Inside was a card with a badge attached, with a big number ten on, plus a twenty-pound note.

Happy birthday to the best son in the world, his dad had written.

'You can phone Dad later and thank him, Trevor.' Trevor nodded. Then his mum gave him two nicely wrapped presents. One was squishy and the other was big and oblong. He peeled the paper off carefully. She had bought him a brand new Xbox, complete with two games, and a fluffy new teddy bear. He hugged his mother fiercely, knowing it must have taken her ages to save up the money for his gifts.

'Wow, thanks, Mum. They're excellent … just what I always wanted,' he lied.

'That's all right, love. Now, go and plug it in – don't ask me how it works, haven't a clue – and I'll start tidying up. Auntie Fiona and Uncle Gary are coming over this afternoon for tea, don't forget. Plus, Neil and Dylan. I expect they'll be able to help you set up your Xbox.'

Neil Braithwaite and Dylan Thompson were in Trevor's class at school and lived on the other side of town. They were nice enough, but outside of school, Trevor didn't know them that well.

'Yes, Mum.' Trevor carried his presents through the hallway and up the stairs. Once in his room, he placed them on the bed, not bothering to open the Xbox or attempt to set it up to his TV. It was while he fiddled with his new teddy's glass eyes that he remembered Desdemona's parting message from the day before:

'You might find something of interest in there.'

He'd forgotten all about it. And she'd told him to check the garden shed first thing in the morning, too! He looked at his bedside clock: 11:15. Still hours till his mid-afternoon birthday tea. He'd go and look now. Trevor wondered if Desdemona had baked him a cake. She made nice cakes, he'd tasted lots. *Hope it's chocolate-flavoured if it is a cake,* he thought.

In moments, Trevor had crept down the stairs and into the lounge. He could hear his mum singing along to the radio in the kitchen. He slid the patio doors open silently and made his way down the garden in his slippers. That was the good thing about slippers, they were brilliant for creeping about in secret. He wondered what spies wore on their feet? *Slippers, probably, but they'd have to be the brown or black, shoe-looking sort – otherwise the secret agents would look really stupid, especially if their bosses made them wear granny tartan ones, with Velcro!* He giggled.

When he reached the shed, Trevor grew inexplicably uneasy. Butterflies bloomed in his stomach and his hands were clammy. *Stop being a plonker,* he scolded himself; *it's a cake!* As his hand closed around the handle, Trevor took a deep breath and quickly pulled open the shed door.

'Mrowl.'

Trevor was good at identifying animal voices and was pretty sure that was a cat. It was gloomy in the shed because ivy grew over the outside, partially obscuring the windowpane. Cautiously, he made his way inside. At first, Trevor couldn't make out where the sound had come from. Then two glowing green orbs hovered in mid-air. He took a step back and stood on something squashy. Looking down, he saw that he'd stepped in poo – in his *slippers!*

'Great,' he said. 'Mum's going to go ballistic!'

'Mrowl,' went the cat voice again.

Squinting towards the green orbs, Trevor saw a black cat as his eyes grew accustomed to the gloom. The green eyes hadn't floated in mid-air at all. The cat sat in a basket on the front of his mum's bike.

Trevor went forward slowly so as not to startle the animal. Tied around the cat's neck was a red ribbon, with a label attached. He reached out and scratched the cat on top of its head. It bent its head towards him, so that Trevor could scratch more easily. 'Ah, aren't you lovely, then,' he said, lifting the large friendly cat out of the basket and taking it over to the open door. He turned the label over to read it.

Midnight

Trevor gulped. He didn't want to cry. He took some deep breaths until he felt under control. Desdemona had only given him his own cat! How amazing was that! And its name was Midnight. And it had a white moon-shaped crescent on its head.

Cool.

Just then, Trevor heard his mum call: 'Trevor! What're you doing out here? Come inside – you can tidy your room for when the boys come over.' He heard her stomp down the garden path.

Trevor started panicking. *She'll go mad if she finds Midnight! What'll I do?*

But he needn't have worried. With a *Pop* (rather like pinging the inside of your mouth with a finger), the cat wasn't there any more!

Instead, sitting in Trevor's cupped palm was a black mouse with the same white moon-mark on its head and a tiny ribbon round its neck. The little creature quickly dove into Trevor's trouser pocket.

'Nothing. Just coming, Mum.' Trevor quickly closed the shed door.

Mrs Talbot stopped right next to her son. 'Urgh! What's that awful smell? Is that you, Trevor?' She wrinkled her nose.

'Um, sorry. I think it's all the excitement, and that,' Trevor said hurriedly.

'Oh, bless your heart.' Mrs Talbot laughed and made her way back up the path to the house. 'I've almost finished the vol-au-vents – just the trifle to make now. You'll have to go easy though, Trevor, if you've got an upset tummy.'

'I will,' called Trevor, dragging his foot along the lawn to wipe off the cat poo. Luckily, it had only stuck to the sole, so by the time he got back to the patio doors his slipper looked quite normal. Walking on tiptoes he snuck to the cupboard under the stairs, found his secret bottle of fabric freshener and gave the slipper a squirt, just to be on the safe side. Then he ran upstairs to his room, careful to cradle the front pocket containing Midnight.

'Out you come.' Trevor removed the silky rodent from his trousers and placed it on the bed where he could admire it. 'How did you change like that? You're no ordinary cat, are you, Midnight?' said Trevor, stating the obvious.

The mouse didn't reply, but began washing its face and ears in a very sweet manner. With another *Pop* it changed back into a cat again, making Trevor jump. Then the animal stretched, lay down, and regarded Trevor with what looked like an amused expression.

'Desdemona gave you to me for my birthday,' said Trevor, 'but I'll have to keep you a secret from Mum. She's not keen on animals, you see … reckons they're more work than they're worth.'

The cat's expression changed suddenly, so that it now looked rather sad.

'I know,' said Trevor. 'Mum never had animals when she grew up. She can't understand why I love them so much.'

At that moment, Mrs Talbot's voice came from the hallway downstairs. 'Trevor! Come and taste this Thousand Island dressing, will you? I'm worried I've put too much paprika in it.'

'Yes, Mum!' yelled Trevor. He turned to the cat. 'Midnight, you're going to have to be quiet and *clean*. We can't have any toilet business in the house, you'll have to hold it in till I let you out later, understand?'

Unbelievably, the cat nodded.

Trevor smiled at his pet's cleverness. 'Good. Well, I have to go, we've got visitors soon and I'm the main attraction.'

At that, Midnight curled up and went straight to sleep.

*

Several long hours later, during which time Trevor had been presented with a new pair of posh trainers by his aunt and uncle; had *Happy Birthday* sung tunelessly at him, and had blown out ten candles embedded in a babyish teddy bear-shaped cake (which made Neil and Dylan giggle and nudge one another); then phoned his dad to thank him for his birthday money, Trevor had just about had enough and was dying to get back to his room to check on Midnight.

'Oh,' said Mrs Talbot, 'I almost forgot. Trevor, take Neil and Dylan upstairs and ask them if they'll set up your Xbox.'

'Aw, but Mum, I–'

'Trevor!' His mum did that starey-eyed, lip-pursing thing at him.

'All right.' Trevor inclined his head and the two boys whooped with delight and thundered past. They waited for him at the top of the stairs.

'Which one's your room?' asked Dylan.

'That one.' Trevor pointed to a door at the end of the landing. 'Just let me–'

Too late, both boys burst through Trevor's bedroom door. He hurried after them, dreading them finding his cat and telling his mum.

'Cool,' said Neil, bouncing on Trevor's bed with his shoes on. 'Massive bed, Trevor!'

Trevor quickly scanned the room for signs of Midnight, but could see nothing out of the ordinary. He let out a long sigh and presumed the cat had become a mouse again, all the better for hiding away.

'Yes,' said Trevor; 'it's King-sized.'

'Lucky you,' said Dylan; 'mine's a red racing car bed. Mum and Dad got it for me when I was three. My feet touch the end now. It's *so* embarrassing. I hate asking friends over. Mum says I can have a new one when I'm ten. Luckily that's only two months away. Can't come soon enough.'

They all laughed, and minutes later the boys had set up the Xbox and were sitting on the floor, trying to defeat an alien horde determined to take over the world.

'Flipping heck!' Neil suddenly leapt off the floor and jumped on the bed. He stared at the corner of the room and pointed.

'What is it?' said Trevor, concerned the game had given Neil the heebie-jeebies.

'There!' cried Neil. '*That* is the hugest, blackest, spider I have *ever* seen!'

Dylan bravely went to the corner of the room and peered up at the ceiling, where a spider the size of a tarantula crouched. 'I love all sorts of insects and arachnids but I've never seen anything like that before … not even in the insect house at the zoo!' He stood on tiptoe to get a better look. 'Wow – it's got some sort of curved white mark on its back!'

'*Midnight,*' Trevor whispered.

'Kill it!' yelled Neil. 'I hate spiders!'

'No!' said Trevor and Dylan together.

'Get rid of it somewhere then.' Neil hid behind a pillow.

'I'll find a container and a sheet of paper and put it out the window,' said Dylan, sensibly.

'N – No,' said Trevor, trying to think. 'It'll get cold.'

Dylan laughed. 'Don't be a numpty, Trevor. Spiders belong outside – and it's summer!' He hurried to Trevor's chest of drawers and emptied pencils and pens out of a china pot; then ripped a sheet of paper from one of Trevor's sketch pads. 'Open the window, Neil.'

Neil just about had enough sense to stumble to the window and fling it open, before flinging himself back on the bed and tucking his legs under him in case the tarantula decided to run up his trouser leg.

Standing on a chair, Dylan guided the very cooperative spider into the pot; then slid the sheet of paper over the opening, trapping it inside. Next he went to the open window, stuck his arms out, removed the paper and gave the pot a good upside-down shake. Cautiously, he peeked inside the pot.

'It's gone,' he said triumphantly.

'Well done, mate,' said Neil, coming over and slapping Dylan on the back. 'Rather you than me. Yuck!' He shivered dramatically.

'Yes … Well done,' muttered Trevor, looking out of the window to see if he could see Midnight. *Great,* he thought, *I've lost my present already! And I didn't even find out whether it was a boy or girl cat. I hope Desdemona won't be too upset. Maybe Midnight's clever enough to go back to the shed?*

'Shut the window, Trevor,' said Neil. 'We don't want that great hairy thing coming back indoors.'

So Trevor reluctantly closed the window and returned to the Xbox.

Later, after the birthday guests had been sent on their way with big wedges of teddy cake wrapped in kitchen roll, Trevor's mum had taken his temperature.
'You look a bit peaky, Trevor.' She peered at the ear thermometer. 'Mm, it says normal. I reckon you'd better have an early night though, don't you? In case you're coming down with something.'

'Okay,' said Trevor, quietly. In truth, he wanted to go to bed and forget about the awful moment Midnight had plummeted to his, or her, probable death. But once there, huddled beneath his duvet, Trevor lay awake for ages and ages.

Happy birthday, Trevor ... not! he thought, miserably.

CHAPTER THREE

Six Times Table

Dragging open his curtains next morning, Trevor was overjoyed to see Midnight sitting outside on his window ledge, casually licking a front paw.

'Midnight,' he murmured, throwing open the window. The cat walked calmly inside and he pulled the animal into his arms, hugging its solid warmth. He mumbled into soft black fur, 'I thought you were dead.'

The cat shook its head.

He placed Midnight on the bed. 'I'd like to know if you're a girl cat or a boy cat, if you don't mind.'

The cat shook its head again.

Trevor studied the large feline closely. 'Boy, I reckon … despite the red ribbon,' he said, certain he was correct.

The cat shook its head once more.

'Girl?'

The cat nodded.

'Oh. A girl.' Trevor stared at Midnight. 'Well, I think I'll take the ribbon off. It's very bright and I'd like you to stay as unnoticeable as possible.'

So Trevor removed Midnight's ribbon and label, storing them away at the back of his underwear drawer. Then he lay down next to the cat, stroking her and marvelling at the perfect moon on her head and the shine of her emerald eyes.
'I think you'd better come to school with me today,' Trevor mused. 'I hate Mondays, it's double maths first thing. And I really don't want to leave you here where Mum might find you.'

Midnight began to purr and in no time at all was fast asleep.

Sighing, Trevor went to the bathroom to brush his teeth. Next, he dressed in his school uniform and went down to breakfast.

Mrs Talbot bustled about in the kitchen. 'I hope you had a nice birthday yesterday, Trevor?' She turned and smiled at Trevor, then came over and gave him a hug.

'Yes, I did. Thanks Mum.'

She planted a wet kiss on his cheek. 'You're such a good boy, Trevor. I'm so lucky to have you. You're no trouble at all.' She picked at a thread on the tea towel she held. 'Sorry you weren't allowed a pet. I know it's what you wanted. You deserve one – you really do. It's just that I don't think I could cope with all the mess of house-training, not to mention the cost of vet bills.'

Trevor blushed. His face felt like it was on fire. 'D – Don't worry, it's all right.'

'Maybe one day, eh?'

'Mm, one day …'

Trevor ate his cereal and drank his orange juice in silence, while his mum finished making his packed lunch. When he'd finished, he jumped up from his chair and dashed into the hallway.

'Where're you off to?' called Mrs Talbot. 'Hurry up, or you'll be late.'

'Forgot something. Won't be a minute!' yelled Trevor, bounding up the stairs two at a time. He threw open his bedroom door to find … nothing. The window was still wide open, but Midnight had disappeared. Trevor tried not to worry. She'd stayed out all night and been perfectly fine. *It's not like she's any old ordinary cat. She probably even knows the Highway Code,* thought Trevor, thinking of all the horrid ways a cat could meet its doom. He sighed and pulled the window almost closed, allowing just enough of a gap for Midnight to get back in if she were a spider.

After saying goodbye to his mum and securing the strap on his cycle helmet, Trevor fetched his bike from the car-port at the side of the house. He climbed on and freewheeled down the path, bumped down the kerb, and cycled out of Forsythia Close. His backpack felt really heavy and he wondered how big a slice of birthday cake his mum had packed for him.

It was as he cycled past the park that Trevor heard a harsh cawing overhead. He looked up quickly. Only a few feet above flew a big black crow. It swooped down and past him, circling the bike.

Then Trevor laughed and whooped.

It *had* to be Midnight: the crow had a funny-shaped white feather on its head.

'Yay, Midnight! You're the best cat in the whole wide world!' And he really thought that, even as an elderly woman walking her arthritic poodle gave him and his flapping, squawking crow a harsh stare. Then Midnight landed on top of Trevor's backpack, making it feel even heavier. 'You weigh a ton!' he yelled, as he cycled along at full pelt. Midnight pulled his earlobe firmly in reply.

'Ouch, Midnight!' he shouted, laughing.

As Trevor approached the school and the herd of children massing through the gateway, Midnight flapped upward into the sky and over the roof.

Trevor locked his bicycle in the bike rack and ran into school. In his classroom he smiled all through registration. When he arrived at his first lesson (the dreaded double maths), Trevor still sat and smiled, prompting another harsh stare, this time from Mr Brunswick, the maths teacher.
'Care to share the joke, Talbot?' The teacher's mouth was set in a thin-lipped tight grimace that was clearly meant to intimidate.

'Um, sorry, I haven't got a joke,' muttered Trevor, blushing and scrabbling to retrieve a maths book from his bag.

'Humph! Good. Maths certainly isn't a subject for humour,' Mr Brunswick went on, 'and to prove it – today we will be concentrating on our times tables.'

The whole class let out a collective groan.

'Quiet!'

Trevor tried to shrink in his seat. Times tables gave him nightmares. He tried, and always failed, to memorise them. Hopefully, Mr Brunswick wouldn't ask him any questions. But usually the teacher never failed to single him out.

'Right, first we'll concentrate on the six times table. Now, I hope you've all been allocating at least an hour a day on this task over the weekend – it's not much to ask, is it, Talbot?'

No, please, not me! 'No, Sir,' said Trevor, weakly.

'Good. Then you won't mind answering the first one, then.' The teacher turned and began to chalk a sum on the blackboard.

As he did, Trevor felt something drop into his lap. He glanced down and saw Midnight, changed to a mouse again. Quickly he looked up at the ceiling to see where she'd come from. Next to a light fitting was a tiny hole.

'Right, Talbot … seven sixes are what, exactly?' Mr Brunswick stared at Trevor with steely narrowed eyes.

Trevor's mouth hung open as he tried to wrack his brain for the answer. 'Seven sixes – seven sixes … It's … um … it's …'

Just when Trevor thought all hope was lost and Mr Brunswick's wrath would befall him, Midnight ran along Trevor's arm and on to the table (luckily, no one seemed to notice). Trevor looked down at Midnight, surprised to see her pick up a pencil that had been sharpened down to half its usual length and write down a number!

'It's forty-two,' said Trevor, confidently.

'It's forty-two,' echoed Mr Brunswick, blinking in surprise and clearing his throat noisily. 'Ahem – yes, that's quite correct … Correctamundo … Well done, Talbot.'

Trevor beamed and the teacher turned his attention to another victim. 'Richardson, what are *nine* sixes?'

*

For the rest of the day, Midnight travelled around safely in Trevor's shirt breast-pocket. At play times he sat at the corner of the playing field in the shade of a tree, reading a book from the school library. Midnight peered from the pocket as though reading the book too.

'Moby Dick,' said Trevor. 'I've read it before. It's one of my favourites.'

Midnight looked up at Trevor with her sparkling blackcurrant eyes and nodded wisely.

'Oh, I suppose you can read too?'

Midnight's whiskers twitched abruptly, twice, which Trevor assumed meant 'Yes'.

'Thanks for helping me out back there in maths,' said Trevor, stroking Midnight's silky head with the tip of a finger.

Midnight carried on reading, so did Trevor, until Moby Dick and Captain Ahab disappeared at last beneath the cold dark sea.

CHAPTER FOUR

Hagcat

The days flew past for Trevor. Midnight had even taken to helping him with his homework. Trevor was amazed that he was beginning to remember his times tables, he would recite them in a sing-song voice to every swing of Midnight's metronome-like tail. Feeding his pet properly had also presented a bit of a challenge at first: Mrs Talbot began buying loads of tins of tuna, which she assumed her son was consuming at an alarming rate. Trevor had had to eat some in front of her too, which was difficult because he despised the stuff. Instead, with his birthday money, he bought a big box of dried cat food at the local shop, which he hid in the shed. He smuggled the pellets inside his pockets when it was time for Midnight's tea and then he told his mum that he'd gone off tuna because he didn't like the fishy smell and could she please stop buying it. She'd sighed then laughed at her awkward son, which had made Trevor feel bad. He hated lying … but he loved Midnight more than not lying …

Saturday morning came around again, and like a lightning bolt striking from a clear sky, Trevor realised he hadn't thanked Desdemona Moles for his birthday gift! The old woman had been vapourised from Trevor's mind at the sheer joy of owning Midnight. He was mortified. *How rude am I!* He blushed to the roots of his red hair at the thought. *Two weeks – two weeks exactly since my birthday!*

He hurriedly dressed and ran the short distance to Desdemona's house. After what seemed like an age for her to answer his knock, the door opened. But it wasn't Desdemona who opened the door. It was Joe. He'd lost a lot of weight since Trevor had seen him last. They stared at one another for what seemed to Trevor to be at least five minutes.

'H – Hello, Joe. Is your mum in?'

'Mum?' said Joe, blankly.

'Yes – I need to speak to her.'

'She's gone to the shop … for bread rolls and a paper,' said Joe, his head brushing the top of the door-frame.

'Oh. Is it all right if I come in and wait then?' Trevor said, realising that was the most he'd heard Joe speak in all the time he'd known him.

Joe waited, his large brown hand patting his trouser leg. 'Mm, okay,' he said at last.

Trevor stepped inside and heard the door clunk shut behind him. He'd never been alone with Joe before. He felt a bit nervous so hurried down the hall and into the kitchen. All the cats dotted around the room turned to stare. He slid onto a kitchen chair. Joe dragged a chair away from the table and sat down heavily.

Trevor smiled.

Joe smiled back, which was the first smile Trevor had ever seen from the man.

Midnight emerged from Trevor's jean's pocket and ran up on to his shoulder.

'Ha, ha!' Joe pointed a sausage-sized finger at the mouse. 'Hagcat!'

'Eh?' said Trevor, frowning.

'Hagcat, that one is.'

Then Midnight leapt, aiming for the table, changing to a cat mid-air and landing silently. She sat on the tablecloth and looked at Joe knowingly.

'Hagcat?' Trevor stared at his pet. 'I've never heard of that before?'

'Mum's cat, Frosty, is one too,' said Joe, inclining his head toward the massive white cat which sat on the very topmost part of the dresser.

Trevor stared at the cat with renewed interest. He'd often admired the animal whenever he visited. And over all her other cats, Frosty always seemed to be closest to Desdemona: draping across the old woman's shoulders like a fur shawl, or curled up in her lap, or lying across her feet – almost always within touching distance.

Just then Joe began humming, then singing, a strange little ditty in a very deep but pleasant voice:

'Our Frosty's not a cat – she's a haaaaagcat,

Never, never ever … a saaaaad cat,

Mouse, bird or dog – never a baaaaad cat,

All the witches in the world got a haaaaagca–'

'Witches!' Trevor interrupted, sitting rigidly upright and staring at Midnight.

'Uh, huh, Mum's been a witch for …' Joe slowly counted his fingers '… all her life.'

Desdemona's a witch! Desdemona's a … witch? 'Your mum's a witch?' Trevor was incredulous.

Joe looked suddenly worried. 'Not a bad one – not bad, Trevor! A good witch is all. Not really s'posed to tell. Med'cine, healing ... makes up nice little spells for the neighbours. Your Midnight's one of Mum's nice little spells, Trevor.'

Midnight gave a bird-like trill and stared at Trevor with her huge emerald eyes.

Trevor sat silently, torn between wanting to run yelling out of the house or hugging Joe half to death at the thrill of it all. Then, just because she could, Midnight went *Pop* and transformed into a beautiful black tufty-eared squirrel. Trevor blinked. Then Frosty went *Ping* and was a fluffy white squirrel, scurrying down the side of the dresser and leaping on to the table to sit beside Midnight. Trevor hadn't noticed before, but Frosty had a little black star on her chest, the same size as Midnight's white moon! *A hagcat ... I've got a hagcat ... A witch's cat!*

'Are normal people like me allowed to have hagcats, Joe?' Trevor was beginning to worry that he might suddenly wake up one morning to find himself wearing a tall black hat and sporting several big warts (even though Desdemona hadn't a wart in sight).

'Well, I'm not sure if they're s'posed to.' Joe's brows furrowed in thought. 'Mum says there are people who've got hagcats but don't know they've got hagcats. A lady Mum knows has got a hagcat but she thinks it's an ordinary normal cat. When Mum was at her house the lady said "There's a funny-looking ginger bird in the garden, it must be one of them foreign ones what's got blown off course, or something" … Course Mum knew straight away it was the lady's own big ginger hagcat.'

Trevor and Joe looked at one another silently for a second before both broke into howls of laughter. Tears streamed down their faces and Joe Moles smacked his hand on the table lots of times. They were still giggling and wiping their eyes when Desdemona came through the front door ten minutes later.

'What's that lovely sound I can hear?' she said, putting her shopping bag on the draining board and leaning her walking stick against the wall in the corner.

'I can't hear anything,' said Joe.

'It's your laughter, my love,' said Desdemona, patting her son on his shoulder. 'It's music to my ears. 'Bout time I heard your laugh again. And well done, Trevor, for bringing the fun in with you.'

'Did I?' said Trevor, amazed at his powers.

'Oh yes – strong medicine, laughter.'

He studied his fingernails. 'I – I came round because I forgot to say thank you for my birthday present. Sorry about that. I really love Midnight.'

Desdemona flapped a hand at him. 'Don't you worry, my boy. You've nothing to be sorry for, though I do appreciate you popping in. I thought you'd be very busy getting to know Midnight. Great timewasters, pets.'

Trevor smiled at the old woman. 'Um, he didn't mean to, but Joe told me that Midnight's a hagcat … a witch's cat.'

Joe sucked in his bottom lip and looked tense.

Trevor went on: 'It doesn't really bother me though; I knew she was special, with all her funny little tricks.' He noticed Desdemona's eyes grow wide for a second, and then relax.

'If I'd known you two lads were going to have a get together I'd have told you all about it myself, Trevor.' She sighed and lowered herself carefully on to a chair. Frosty immediately turned from a squirrel into a cat and curled up on her mistress's lap. 'But it really doesn't matter. I wanted you to have a *knowing* pet because of your mother's, um, reluctance. Thought Midnight might help you keep the secret, sort of thing. Your mum hasn't found out has she, Trevor?'

'Oh no, hasn't got a clue – but I do feel a bit guilty, you know, about lying to her.'

'But it's only a white lie, isn't it, Mum?' said Joe, smiling broadly at his mother.

'Yes, Joe, it is. But probably she'll find out about Midnight one day, hopefully not for a long, long time,' said Desdemona. 'So, what was all the giggling about when I came in?'

Trevor told Desdemona that they'd been laughing about the ginger bird, and in no time Desdemona was laughing too, and going into greater detail: 'That's my friend's hagcat, Mumfy. He's got a white lightning mark down his back to set him apart too, but how he's kept from changing in front of her shows such remarkable restraint. I wish Mumfy would stop winking at me whenever he sees me though; she keeps taking him to the vet convinced there's something wrong with his eyes!'

Then they were laughing again, laughing and laughing until their faces ached and their sides hurt, and so the cake tin was opened, and several mugs of hot chocolate and slices of Battenberg later, it was time for Trevor to take himself and Midnight home for lunch.

'I won't be able to eat a thing after all that nice cake,' said Trevor, going to the front door, 'but I'll have to force myself, otherwise Mum'll think I'm ill.'

'I'm sure you'll manage,' said Desdemona, following. 'And thanks again, Trevor, for bringing some sunshine into the house. Joe's been so down since … you know, Dreadnought.'

'That's all right,' said Trevor, blushing.

'We're going to the rescue centre tomorrow, to look at some dogs. Joe wasn't keen but I think a new dog will help fill the space in both their lives.'

'Oh that's nice,' said Trevor. 'Um, and, I'd like to say, I really don't mind having a witch for a friend.'

'I'm so glad,' Desdemona said, smiling.

Trevor's brow furrowed as he thought of something else. 'So, Desdemona …'

'Yes, Trevor.'

'… Do you fly on a broomstick?'

She laughed. 'No, no. Not with my hip! The local bus suits me just fine.'

'Right. Okay. Well, see you then.'

'See you, Trevor, and pop in any time at all.'

'I will.'

CHAPTER FIVE

Jamaican Spice

Oh rats, Trevor thought, *it doesn't look like I'll be popping anywhere any time soon!*

His mum stood in the kitchen with one hand on her hip and the other … holding a big box of cat food!

'Look what I found in the shed, Trevor,' said Mrs Talbot, trying to keep her voice as level as possible, 'along with some old cat poo! Where do you think this magically came from?'

'Um,' said Trevor, gulping, 'the shop I expect.'

'The shop! And I wonder who bought it?'

Trevor was sure there was steam coming from his mum's ears and that it wasn't his imagination. 'It – It was me,' he said.

His mum slammed the box on the kitchen table. She had a flaming patch of red on each cheek. 'Trevor, I'm so disappointed! You've been hiding a cat from me, haven't you? And there's no use denying it – there was black hair all over your duvet cover!'

Trevor's shoulders slumped. The game was up; already. From now on he decided to tell the truth. He sighed. 'I – I'm sorry, Mum. I didn't mean to hide her from you – but she was a birthday present.'

'She?'

'My hag– I mean my cat, Midnight.'

'Midnight, is it? I see. And where is this cat?'

Trevor felt Midnight squirm in his pocket. 'She's … ah … hidden herself somewhere at the moment, I think.'

'Has she?' said Mrs Talbot, closing her eyes and shaking her head. 'Well, she'd better hide herself somewhere permanently! I – am – not – having – pets – in – this – house! Understand!'

Tears sprang into Trevor's eyes and rolled down his cheeks. 'Yes, Mum.'

'And which bright spark gave you a cat, then?'

Trevor panicked, even though he'd vowed he wouldn't lie again. 'N – No one, I found her at the park!'

'You just told me you got her for your birthday!'

'No, I – it's just that–'

'It's that Moles woman isn't it! She's given you a cat without asking my permission first. A blinking cheek, I call it!' Trevor's silence and stricken expression told Mrs Talbot that her assumption was correct. 'Come on – we're going round there right now to sort this mess out!'

'I can't, Mum. It wouldn't be very polite …' Trevor protested feebly.

But his mum grabbed his hand and led him out of the house. Seconds later she hammered on the Moles' front door.

As if she'd known all along that someone would soon be knocking, Desdemona immediately opened the door. 'Mrs Talbot – Trevor, how nice to see you both. Won't you come in, please?'

'Thank you,' said Mrs Talbot through tightly pursed lips. She towed Trevor inside.

'Go straight through to the kitchen, Mrs Talbot,' said Desdemona, closing the door and following her visitors down the hall.

In the kitchen, Mrs Talbot stood with her back to the wall and held Trevor in front of her like a shield. She stared at Desdemona's cats in horror. 'Oh, my word! What a lot of cats!' She immediately began scratching her head, as if she'd caught fleas.

'Lovely, aren't they? Each and every one has a special place in my heart. And do please call me Desdemona, Mrs Moles is so impersonal.' Desdemona went to the fridge and took out some milk. 'How about a mug of lovely cocoa?'

'Ah, no – no thank you,' said Mrs Talbot. 'I've brought Trevor round because he's been keeping a cat in his room against my express wishes … And it appears that you gave the animal to him. I'm really very cross about it. You'll have to take the cat back straight away Mrs … Desdemona.'

But Desdemona poured milk into a saucepan anyway, and took a tin of cocoa from one of her cupboards. Silently she lit the stove and placed the pan of milk on the flames; then added several large spoonfuls of cocoa powder and brown sugar. Stirring the mixture, she turned back to Mrs Talbot and Trevor and smiled, flashing dazzling gold teeth. 'All problems seem insignificant after a nice chocolate beverage, I find.'

'Um, yes, well, be that as it may. Trevor,' Mrs Talbot turned Trevor around to face her, 'in a minute you'll go and find what's-its-name–'

'Midnight.'

'–That's right, Midnight, and bring her back to Desdemona, please. And no arguing!'

'Yes, Mum.' Trevor continued to weep silent tears, brushing them angrily off his cheeks every few seconds.

Desdemona laughed. 'I'm sure Trevor doesn't need to go traipsing around trying to look for his cat when he's got her in his pocket all along. Do you, Trevor?' The old woman looked meaningfully at him.

'N – No, Desdemona,' said Trevor, worried about where this was going.

'In his pocket?' sneered Mrs Talbot. 'Really, please stop with all this nonsense. It's a real cat, not a little toy. A real cat eats real cat food. And toy cats don't leave poo in my shed!'

'Oh, that really was naughty of Midnight,' said Desdemona, frowning.

'It was my fault,' mumbled Trevor, 'I didn't find her till later on.'

'Not to worry – come out and show yourself, Midnight.'

Trevor looked at the old woman, alarmed. 'No!' he blurted. But even as he said the words he could feel Midnight wriggling towards his pocket-opening. Then she climbed up his jumper and sat on his shoulder.

'But it's a mouse!' exclaimed Mrs Talbot.

'No, she's definitely a cat,' corrected Desdemona.

A single *Pop* later and Midnight purred contentedly, delicately draped herself across Trevor's shoulders and stared into Mrs Talbot's wide eyes.

'It – It–' Mrs Talbot's mouth opened and closed repeatedly, like a fish out of water. She fumbled for the back of a chair and leant heavily against it before sitting down. She stared at the cat, unable to drag her eyes from the animal.

Trevor sighed. 'Don't be scared, Mum. Midnight's not an ordinary cat. She's what they call a hagcat. She's special, that's why Desdemona gave her to me. She helps me with my maths' He smiled encouragingly.

But his mum seemed incapable of speech. Her eyes bulged and she'd gone very pale. Trevor hoped she wasn't going to pass out.

'Right, I think the cocoa's ready now,' said Desdemona, pouring steaming thick chocolate into three mugs. She went to the dresser and scanned all the little bottles and jars; then selected a red glass bottle and took it over to the mugs. Next she turned her back, so that no one could see her tip a tiny amount of amber-coloured liquid into one mug before stirring it. 'Here we go,' she said, beaming, as she placed a big mug of cocoa in front of Mrs Talbot.

Trevor's mum stared at the cocoa as if she didn't know what it was.

'Drink it, Mum,' said Trevor. 'They reckon something sweet's like medicine when you've had a shock.'

Mrs Talbot nodded blankly and picked up the mug with two shaking hands. She took a sip, then another, before wrinkling her nose. 'Mm, very hot,' she murmured. 'And spicy, burning my tongue … Tastes strange.'

Desdemona brought the other two mugs of chocolate to the table and indicated that Trevor should sit down, so he did, with Midnight still balanced across his shoulders.

Some colour crept back into Mrs Talbot's face.

'I just added a little Jamaican spice to your chocolate, that's all,' said Desdemona, winking at Trevor. 'Come along – drink up.'

In another minute or so, Trevor's mum had drained her mug. She looked at the cats all around the room. 'Exactly how many cats do you have, Desdemona?' she asked calmly.

'Nineteen at the moment,' said Desdemona, 'but I never know when that number will change. Cats sometimes have a way of finding their homes for themselves. Perhaps tomorrow, or the day after, I might well be adding another to the list.'

To Trevor's surprise, his mum actually smiled.
'Some of them are rather pretty, aren't they?' said Mrs Talbot.
'Apart from that one, over there.' She nodded toward a tabby cat lying on the window-sill, whose ears were in tatters and whose coat had big bald patches.

'That's Peter the Great,' said Desdemona, laughing. 'At twenty-three he's allowed to look a bit past his best.'

Mrs Talbot's brow furrowed. 'But I did see Trevor's cat change, didn't I? I wasn't imagining it?'

Desdemona smiled. 'No, you weren't imagining anything.' The old woman then went on to tell Mrs Talbot all about the history of hagcats and their place in the twenty-first century, how they were quite scarce and how they'd been unfairly persecuted through the ages; then she told her how pets were good for children and taught them compassion and responsibility. 'So, I'm afraid you have somewhat a duty of care towards Midnight, Mrs Talbot.'

'How's that?'

'It's like this,' Desdemona went on, 'you see, I performed a little … *charm* on the cat, which has bound her to your son for as long as one or the other shall live.'

Mrs Talbot looked from Trevor, to Midnight, and back again. 'I see,' was all she said for a moment.

Trevor held his breath and sat as still as a statue. Midnight stopped purring too, and seemed to be waiting for something to happen.

Trevor's mum let out a long sigh. 'Yes, well, you have to make sure you look after her properly, Trevor …'

'I will,' said Trevor, overjoyed.

'… And clean up after her. We'll ask Dad if he wouldn't mind contributing towards vaccinations.'

Trevor leapt up and threw his arms around his mum's neck. 'Oh thank you – thank you so, so, much!'

Midnight's face pressed against Mrs Talbot's cheek and the hagcat licked it.

'Ooh,' giggled Mrs Talbot, 'that's enough Midnight. Let's not get carried away, eh?'

Trevor went back to his chair and Midnight pummelled his lap with her front paws and lay down.

Shortly after, Joe came down stairs and joined them in the kitchen. If he was surprised to see Mrs Talbot, he didn't show it. 'I was on the internet. I think I've picked one I like at the rescue centre,' he said to Desdemona. 'He looks special.'

'Oh that's good, Joe,' said his mother. 'What breed is he?'

'Not sure?' said Joe, frowning.

'Never mind, we'll soon find out tomorrow. Mug of chocolate, Joe?'

'No thanks, Mum. I'm a bit fed up with cocoa.'

Trevor and Desdemona laughed. Mrs Talbot joined in a little bit too, just to be polite but she hadn't a clue why.

Later, as they were leaving, Trevor whispered to Desdemona: 'What did you put in Mum's cocoa?'

Desdemona bent close to his ear. 'A little drop of acceptance – that's all.'

'Oh.' Trevor didn't know what that was, but it was powerful stuff, that was for sure.

*

The following evening Trevor was on his way to the park. Midnight was in the guise of a gorgeous sleek pointer-type dog. It was the first time she'd made the transformation and Trevor was delighted he had a dog to finally play 'fetch' with.

'Wait for me, Trevor!' called a deep voice from behind him.

Trevor turned around. Running towards him was Joe, being pulled along by a big Dalmatian.

'Wow, Joe. So you got him then?'

'Yep,' said Joe, out of breath from the short sprint. 'You'll never guess what he is though. Look very closely.'

Intrigued, Trevor studied the dog. Only after a minute or so had passed did he finally realise. 'He's a *hagcat!* That black mark on his back's in the shape of a cobweb! Cool!'

That day would be the start of many adventures for Trevor, Midnight, Joe, and Spider. The park turned into a wonderful world of cowboys and round-ups, aliens and spacemen, building dens and running from terrifying werewolves, being shipwrecked and saving the world from zombies. Nothing was impossible, ever again.

And Mrs Talbot had grown very fond of Midnight, too. Especially when she'd come home from an outing to find the hagcat sliding carefully along the mantelpiece with a duster between her front paws.

'You know,' she said to Trevor one evening, 'I really can't imagine life without Midnight. This place feels like a proper home now. It's so strange … It's as if she's cast a spell over me or something.'

Midnight curled up on Mrs Talbot's lap and allowed the woman to stroke her. Then the hagcat stared straight at Trevor and winked.

Writing For Dogs

By

Lyn Flanders

Lyn lives in Scotland with her husband Phillip and is a long time animal rescuer and carer. She is a first time author who has contributed a piece detailing the trials and tribulations of a certain period of her life and the sacrifices both she and her husband made, all in the name of animal welfare and protection.

The dangers of spontaneity

It is the dream of many to escape to the country attracted by the idea of a life of peace and tranquillity. There are those who believe in the myth that country life is idyllic. I was never one of them and after our experience never will be.

Purely by chance I had picked up a `Property Guide` whilst queuing in the bank and glanced idly at the pages. We were extremely happy in our beautiful Newport home and had no plans to move at all. Our house was a comfortable spacious Victorian villa which we had fallen in love with on first sight. It sat high above the river with a stunning uninterrupted view of the `Tay`, the two bridges and the Sidlaw and Perthshire hills making up the backdrop. The sunsets were terrific and a permanent tripod sat at the lounge window for many years to capture some of the stunning evening skies. At night time the reflection of the coloured lights from the city of Dundee which was directly opposite made for a view we could never tire of seeing. We had lived here happily for fourteen years improving it as we went and caring for our cats and tortoise as well as fostering continually for homeless cats and kittens.

We bought it when our daughter Vikki was about to start secondary school. The big attraction was that it came with two thirteen year old cats, a magnificent big longhaired black and white boy Sweep and his brother Tiger, a big tabby boy. We had always wanted cats but neighbours in our previous home which had open plan gardens made it plain they were anti-cats so I did not hesitate to offer to keep the old boys already living there, especially when I was rewarded on our first visit to view with a big longhaired black and white fluffy Sweep on my lap!

His brother Tiger was a big tabby and white gentleman who favoured Vikki from the moment he met her so we were well pleased to take over their care. They had previously been restricted to sleeping in the porch but now we promoted them to our bedroom at night time. They were adorable and Sweep was a well known character in the terrace for lying in the middle of the road and failing to move for traffic. My worry that he would be hit was unfounded. Sadly Sweep died a few months after a short middle ear infection and we experienced the grief that losing our first cat brings.

Vikki was returning from a stay in France and I well remember driving to the airport and sobbing all the way. My red tearstained face was a giveaway and when she saw me she too burst into tears. Yes, we were all in mourning for this wonderful boy.

Tiger lived another four years and was seventeen when we were gifted a Brown Burmese kitten Benji. Knowing this little cat would not be welcomed by Tiger and we initially refused him but Benji was foisted upon us as if we had no say. Tiger was furious! The last thing he needed at his time of life was a playful kitten jumping on him! The day he arrived was Phillip`s birthday and to solve the problem, and give Phil a special birthday gift, we went out and bought another kitten! Being pre-Cats Protection days we paid fifty pence for a semi feral kitten from the Dundee pet store.

Phil chose him from a cage containing a litter of cute grey and white kittens. He was bigger than the rest and not a sibling. He was black but covered in long white hairs giving him the impression of looking like a little old man. He was hiding at the back of the cage looked rather dirty and his large feet were impacted with sawdust!

We called him Scamp and loved him despite his reluctance to befriend us. He was the ideal companion for Benji and the two kittens played well together leaving Tiger to sleep all day in peace! The three boys lived in harmony until Tiger died and we were once again back to two cats. Benji was a very intelligent cat but Scamp was thick as a plank! My next door neighbour Ray was very fond of our cats and she adored Benji. He was so clever and people friendly and often jumped the adjoining wall to visit her whilst we were out at work. One day the postie had covered the cat flap with a big parcel barring Benji's way indoors. He went round to Ray and made it plain that she should follow him home! She saw his problem right away and solved it for him by moving the parcel! My clever cat!!

With the intention of increasing the cat family further I set off one day for Glencarse Cat Sanctuary and chose a beautiful longhaired tabby and white boy kitten. As I was leaving I spotted a tiny black boy and asked when he would be ready! `Oh they are brothers– he is ready now! ` So off I went carrying the cat basket with two lovely kittens inside. I now know better but then I went home excitedly waving the cat carrier – `look who I have brought for you`!!! Scamp was timid and curious but Benji was FURIOUS!! In an instant he changed from the sweet endearing boy we knew into a raging vicious tiger! He hated the kittens with a vengeance and as the days passed instead of becoming used to them and accepting their presence he became worse and more aggressive.

As luck would have it my lovely neighbour Maureen offered the kittens a home and they went off happily with their saviour! She named them Pablo and Lenny – after Picasso and De Vinci! As soon as Benji realised they had gone for good he immediately relaxed, stopped his tantrums and we all sighed with the relief of being back to one happy family.

When Benji was killed aged five on the main road which was two streets away from our house we were devastated.

I realised that since we had sampled how delightful they were I could not live without a Burmese cat. I needed another in my life and I had noticed an advert in the local paper the weekend before Benji departed this world. A fifteen week old Brown Burmese boy Koko! I hauled out the paper and phoned the owners and two hours later we welcomed Koko to our home - one timid introvert boy – as far removed from Benji as could be! Nervous of people he was happy to see another one of his own kind and he and Scamp were soon playing happily together. He and I never had the relationship of my previous boy but we cared for him dearly as we would any cat.

Phil had just started a part time MBA at Dundee University. Vikki had gone off to Stirling University. I was all of a sudden a redundant mum. She had always said if you didn`t meow in our house you got no attention so she took herself off and as I recall never came back! Well that`s a bit of exaggeration – she did reappear for holidays and short breaks but was independent enough to get her own place and a job in Edinburgh when she graduated so was never dependant on us again. I am extremely proud of her and though she recognised my passion for cats I can assure you readers I am a totally devoted mum.

Cats rule ok!

By chance – as everything seems to be with my life – I happened to be in town one day, it was October 1987, when I happened to go to a coffee morning which was being run by Cats Protection.

Almost before I knew it I was invited to join the few volunteers who were doing their best for the Dundee stray and unwanted cats. My first visit to the `shelter` left me sad. There were about twenty cats in a stone outhouse within the garden of a local business woman. In those days they had one communal room – I shudder to think of it now – but it gave them a roof and food and I have since seen far worse sights. I got home that day and burst into tears. I hated to see those little innocent faces locked up without heat or light at night and vowed there and then to help as many as I could!

The first of the homeless to join our feline family was Gabby the tabby. She was an unwanted longhaired tabby kitten with a lovely nature and became instant friends with Scamp and Koko. She had many escapades but the daddy of them all was when she went missing and during an extensive search I discovered her one evening on the roof of the local old folk`s home! Forty feet off the ground and as the crow flies 100 yards from our house. To carry out his rescue attempt Phil had to walk 300 yards round the roads carrying a heavy ladder!

When he got there and discovered the ladder was too small I panicked and called on the local fire brigade. To their credit they came charging down from Tayport all blue lights flashing. By now it was dark and the elderly residents were getting ready for their beds. In and out of various rooms charged the fire crew, the old people now hanging out of windows to see what the fuss was about! They located the room above which stood our Gabby. I was extremely embarrassed and relieved when she was caught and safely lowered to the ground in a basket. We thanked everyone profusely and trotted off home with the naughty high flyer!

The next day I looked up to see that she really could have made her own way back down, the same way as she had no doubt got up! When she went missing again and I checked the roof of the `Seymour` there she was back on top! I ignored her this time and she soon reappeared back home! Phew! One of the residents had reported the incident to the local newspaper but had been confused about Phil`s part. The report contained a sentence wrongly saying Mr Flanders had brought a ladder but was too afraid to climb it! ` I still cringe today at the memory!

By this time I had become renowned in our village as the `cat woman`. The phone rang incessantly with calls regarding cats. Missing and found cats and kittens became a regular occurrence. A dear little biscuit coloured boy of around six weeks old was found on the railway and brought to me. Goodness knows how he got there. I called him Skimmy after T.S.Elliot`s Skimbleshanks and positively adored him. There was a weakness about him that endeared him to me but we cannot keep them all and if there was no reason other than my love then it was better he went to a home of his own. Thinking otherwise one can easily become a hoarder and that is unfair on the other cats. One day a lovely lady I had not met before walked into the library asking me about this kitten. She had been referred by our local vet. After a few questions about her lifestyle I knew instinctively this was the right home for him. There was only a gentle black lab at home as well as a husband who did not mind a cat coming into the home. A home check proved it was indeed a welcoming loving home for Skimmy.

I had sized up the option of keeping him but as it should be I made his welfare a priority and knew he would get far more attention as a sole cat. I spent the next three weeks crying for him. Some get deep into your heart very quickly and I always missed this baby. He had been in his home for a few months when I got a call to say he was missing. For a cat who never went out of the garden I was amazed and suspected he might well be very near home. I set a trap within the garden and was proved right when he turned up soon after attracted by the smell of the food. Turned out he was slightly brain damaged and was never really a normal cat but was a couthy boy who plodded along doing his own thing. He opted for a quiet life and chose to be a house cat. He died aged sixteen and I cried again for this cat who had a good life but I still wished it had been with me.

Another who came our way but *did* stay was a longhaired tortoiseshell girl aged around six months. She turned up at the old folks` home in Newport and I set a trap for her as I was told she ran away whenever approached. Caught in the trap I took her straight to the vet for assessing and neutering but when I looked at her little face and huge dark eyes I knew I could not let her go! She turned out to be just a frightened domestic cat and as gentle as could be. We called her Tiggy Mary and she had a lovely long eighteen years with us.

I soon had the dubious pleasure of being Coordinator of Dundee Cats Protection League. We continued to admit and rehome hundreds of cats from the old house in Broughty Ferry Road but it was not ideal. We now had a few rows of wooden pens and had installed heating but we slid around in the mud a lot. We needed lots of things but we were desperate for new premises. To that end I visited Councillor Ian Luke at his open surgery every Saturday for weeks on end and plagued him with requests to find somewhere suitable for our group to house cats. Eventually it paid off. I am sure he was fed up seeing me week after week and my persistence had worn him down. However it happened we became the proud tenants of the current building in Foundry Lane. It has since been transformed and upgraded to a spotlessly clean cattery with charity shop attached and a big bright office and reception. Many thousands of cats have since passed through its doors since its conception and conditions for the cats are the best they have ever had!

My day job as a Training Officer was an outdoor job enabling me to drop into the cat shelter at odd times of the day. The charity work took over my life and every waking hour was spent one way or another with the re-homing of cats and kittens.

I recently met up with my old boss who reminded me that I would get a call to go rescue a cat somewhere and off I would rush no matter what work commitments – I am sure she was exaggerating! The next cat to come to us was Jenny Anydots. I saw her owner drop her off at the cattery one morning. She was being carried in a yellow cellular blanket and her eyes were popping out of her head in fear and trembling. Work took me to Aberdeen that day but her eyes never left me! I picked her up on the way home and she promptly ran up the floor to ceiling bookshelves and stayed there all night!

She stayed with us for over a year until life became unbearable for her being bullied by the other cats. We found her a quiet home with a family whom had no other pets and offered her a stress free life.

My heart goes out to those timid cats brought to rescue centres and shelters every day. The more timid the longer they will be stuck in their prison as most people want friendly cuddly pets.

The Crieff Rescues

The saddest cats in the world are the ferals. Through no fault of their own, circumstances have let them breed and become very afraid of humans. Individually they are just as lovely as domestic cats but suffer dreadfully due to being forced to fend for themselves. There are a few human friends of ferals who trudge the streets feeding those unfortunate cats many of whom could be domesticated with time and patience.

One day we were notified of an injured black and white girl in a colony in Crieff. Living in King Street Car Park and known as Blackie by her loyal feeder. Mary Ford told us her tail was in a dreadful state of decay – half had dropped off and she badly needed help. I went off to trap her with the intention of taking her straight to our vet but a few attempts later and I still had not managed to catch her. This became a routine 100 mile round trip with the aim of catching Blackie but although she evaded the trap we caught many of her offspring whom we had neutered and returned.

I was sad to return them to the rotten habitat where they existed beneath an old building adjoining King Street car park but at least here they had the lovely Mary to feed them daily. And so it became a 200 mile round trip leaving at five in the morning then trapping, taking back to our Dundee vet to be neutered and returned later that day. This went on for a number of weeks and I think I clocked up 3000 miles but still did not ensnare Blackie. Then I heard of a trapper extraordinaire – Sue Hancock. Sue had moved up to Scotland from Manchester with 48 cats and lived on a big farm in Fife. She was an organised and patient trapper – both essential qualities. Within a week Sue had caught the evasive cat but sadly by then the poison had gone into her bloodstream. She died in captivity of septicaemia.

My failure to trap Blackie had led me to having a crate type trap made by one of our volunteers. First time we tried it out – with one of us sitting behind bushes holding the end of a long string to pull it shut – along came a dog!! This was early morning and the poor boy was dirty and starving. It shot into the crate and scoffed the cooked chicken! Well we couldn't leave it there so into the car and back to the cattery to assess it for cat friendliness! Had it shown no interest in cats I might then have had my first dog but as it was he was all for chasing them.

A phone call later and he went to one of my friends Brenda to be fostered. I had reported the find to the Crieff police and to the local dog rescues. One week later I had a phone call from a young chap saying I had his dog. Now had he phoned the day I found the dog I would have been far happier but anyone leaving it a week before looking for his dog did not impress me one bit. I asked him to describe the dog and sadly it did seem to belong to him. He told us the dog`s name and that his child was pining for him so I agreed to take the dog back to him in Crieff next day. Brenda said he was a marvellous dog who had been biddable and friendly.

We drove off with him being cuddled in the back seat by Brenda. As we reached Crieff he started to quake and quiver. We drove down the main street and I stopped fairly near the address the young man had given with the intention of handing him over. At that moment a young woman walking past stopped and spoke to the dog. She told us she was sad to see him back as he kept running away due to being beaten in his home. `He has a rotten life there` she said. I had heard enough to decide to turn around and take him back! Well he visibly relaxed as we drove out of Crieff and despite threats and abusive calls I rehomed the lovely natured dog to a very nice family back in Fife! You might think this was wrong but I would always protect any animal in a bad situation and I will fight tooth and nail for their rights.

We continued to trap and neuter the rest of the colony and one snowy day a very hungry tabby and white boy appeared and started munching a bowl of food I had put down. He had the thinnest tail I have ever seen and he obviously was unable to afford a decent winter coat. As he ate I touched his head with my fingers and he did not flinch. A true feral would not let you within feet of them and I knew I could rehabilitate this boy.

I took him home with me that day. I converted the big garden shed into a cosy palace for him and spent the following two months lying on my front in the big garden shed feeding titbits of roast chicken and chatting gently to this young boy who was now Sweet William and who would be adored by our family until he was eleven and died of a crumbling spine.

One stormy night the wind was howling. I could not leave this little cat alone in the shed so took a cat carrier out with me and with using gauntlets managed to get him into the wicker basket. Indoors to warmth and comfort we came. He immediately crawled behind the bed in the foster room and I left him to it and went off for a well-earned sleep. He turned out to be the most adorable loving cat who would sleep clinging to my head like a close fitting hat. It was a bit alarming at first with sharp claws resting on my forehead. From car park to cosy bed – nothing pleased me more than turning a life around.

To make life easier when integrating cats we had glass doors made for all the rooms set around the hall. All the cats could see each other and by mixing their scents and taking their time integration was relatively easy. William was indoors to stay and became a very happy boy who liked nothing better than a lap! Many of these so called feral cats have formerly been domesticated and time and patience can restore their trust but not many people have the time or the will to devote to this end.

When William died ten years later I thought I would die with the pain of his loss. I loved this boy so very much. But the price of love is the grief we suffer when we lose them, I have since been there many times but it never becomes any easier.

In fact the less time they are with me the worse it can be. I had brought home a very matted longhaired boy from Tayport after a call for help. He had been straying and was in very neglected state. His coat was white with dark patches and I called him Mr Mottle. The people who reported him had said he was wild but by evening this poor soul was lying on my chest purring like a motor engine. He was a darling. Just one week after he arrived I heard him scream and rushed to find out what was wrong. I was shocked to see puddles of blood all over the carpet. Neither he nor the carpet recovered and the vet reckoned he had internal tumours which had burst. I was inconsolable. This poor boy who had been struggling to survive had missed his chance of a more comfortable life and there was nothing we could do about it. If I had been able to turn the clock back for him I would, but death has no dominion!

The cat family was growing at home. By now we had in addition a pair of twins Samantha and her sister Poppy, two darling black and white unwanted teenagers, and Gnasher - a character we had brought home one weekend as he had skinned his nose on the chicken wire in his pen. He was five months old and not one to be contained. He had slid at top speed into a factory on Kingsway – one of the busiest Dundee roads and from there he was brought to the cattery. Phil felt sorry for his nose and so he had landed himself a home for the night! He had jumped up on the sofa between the two sisters and no one said boo and so he stayed!

He was a great boy who loved any kittens we were fostering and was a good dad to them all. One such kitten was handed into us one Sunday morning. Phil had come to help me do cleaning duties and a woman arrived clutching a shoe box in which lay a five inch long grey kitten. She had rescued him from a feral colony where the father had killed another. With just the two of us there we could not go and leave this tiny morsel and so brought him home to be the first kitten I would hand rear! Of course we could not part with him and so he became a big part of our family and was adored by us all. Vikki came home for a holiday and played a large part in his upbringing! She proudly taught him to use the litter tray at three weeks old and he never looked back.

Montreathmont beckons

Through the Cats Protection League (as it was at the time – now called just Cats Protection) I met hundreds of people and made many friends along the way. I was accused, fairly I imagine, of cornering everyone I met and gently convincing them that what they needed was a cat. As I met many people through my work I was able to home many cats and kittens. I spent my days either elated when our little homeless souls got homes or deflated when they languished, usually over the summer months, in pens. Innocent animals imprisoned through no fault of their own!

Amongst these who suffered a long incarceration were five feral cats who had been displaced when Invergowrie paper mill closed down. Stuck in our shelter for many months they were a constant worry to me.

As I read that property guide in the bank, the word `PADDOCK` leapt out at me. I read on, a country cottage with an acre, paddock and many outhouses and it dawned on me that I could give these five a home. I couldn't wait to share this brainwave with the family! I called my daughter Vikki and dragged her off to view the property. I did not think of it as a bad omen then but there was a crash on the main road leading to the place and we were held up for half an hour whilst they cleared it and we got going again. Being 26 miles from home and the sole house in the forest seemed neither isolated nor a deterrent.

A rusty old sign at the end of a private road announced we had arrived at Montreathmont Cottage 200 yards at the end of which stood a white painted cottage. Set back a few feet from the road alongside a huge grassy area, which could not be called a lawn, surrounded by high trees and beyond that the large paddock. To the right of the cottage were a number of sheds and a huge barn, beyond which was a large boat. There was no formal garden, just a huge area of lumpy grass and - being May - huge clumps of daffodils around the foot of the tree nearest the house. There was also a lot of goose dirt everywhere underfoot, but nothing was a deterrent that day!

The next bad omen came when I fell down the few deep steps which led to the front door - right into the arms of the owner, an unsavoury character in camouflage clothing. He was more than happy to show us around and was a bit surprised when I asked to see the outhouses first, a selection of sheds in varying stages of decay and none secure enough to hold a feral cat. The large barn had prominent holes in the ceiling, little did I know then the damage that was to occur to all our furniture in this hole peppered hangar!

He introduced us to the birds which would be staying – two geese, six hens and a cockerel. They each had their own housing, rather smelly and like everything else in need of repair and renovation. The man himself was interested in old cars and we subsequently found a number of these in bits and buried below ground.

I would love to say a pool lay to the left of the house but it was just a pond. The view from the front of the house was of the huge duck pond belonging to the farmer. Dozens of ducks quacked away happily and I had no idea at that moment that in a few months these lovely fellows would all be shot dead by the visiting Italians tourists.

The house was a small cottage which had been extended. The main cottage would have originally been a but 'n ben and was 150 years old. Added to it was a back hallway, bathroom and bedroom. Everything was grubby but I could see past the dirt and, being always up for a challenge, imagined how it would look once we had renovated the place. Most of the walls were clad in old wood panelling except for the room containing a big black range where the wall was non existent but instead a huge piece of tartan fabric was nailed to the posts. Little point in making comparisons but against my lovely wallpapered solid walls back home it didn't stand a chance. However, it had potential!

Some of the history was known and we heard that long ago a local called Granny Todd had lived there for many years. I am now sure her ghost remained there and probably still is. I have no idea how she died but she was not a happy ghost and certainly not at all pleased by our presence. I am sure she had decided to make my life unbearable because never in my life had I been made to feel so miserable.

The paddock which had excited me was huge, lumpy underfoot and contained Daisy and Archie the geese although they had no names until we named them. There was no running water near them and it became the first task of the day carting over buckets full of water for the geese.

There was also a small paddock which contained the hen house and this too was pretty rough ground. Behind the house and forming part of the garden was a hill covered in primrose and along with the daffodils looked bright and lovely. Being of a romantic nature and an idiot these served to cover my eyes to the miserable conditions and I pictured myself sitting upon this little hill which had an all-round view, sketch pad in hand! Silver birch trees lined the skyline and I could picture Phil and myself strolling round the garden on a summer evening enjoying the peace and quiet and the animals. We would have the house sorted and upgraded and life would be idyllic. Or so we thought then!

Vikki was horrified! She pointed out it was a dump and the house was awful and it was too far from all our friends and my work and went on about how I was a people person and would be lonely out there, especially as Phil worked away from home a lot! She had almost convinced me I would be making a big mistake but when Phil came home that evening I was so enthusiastic that he agreed to go back with me to see for himself.

The owner obviously could not believe his eyes when he saw me back there. The goose dirt had not put me off – I was made of sterner stuff!! When Phil saw the size of the garden and the stone staircase leading down to the stream – along with the old well and water pump he got caught up in my excitement too, I thought! By the time I had dragged him up the hill and through the primrose path he was also thinking we could do this. We went into the caravan – old and dilapidated – which could be the hide where we could watch the deer in our garden and that just about clinched it. We would be down sizing but we didn't really need all the rooms we had, did we? At that crucial moment in time a deer happened by the garden and that was the signal we needed! We decided we would go for it!

The survey contained the small word 'damp'. Hardly noticeable as a word but the implications were huge. Mad beings that we are we went ahead. It was to be our own little estate and would give us the chance to help more animals than ever – or so I thought!

Our own beautiful home had sold right away. I picked up the massive key for the ancient door of our new home – the stone slab below it had worn down leaving a gap of a couple of inches. We later saw this was a handy entrance for the tiny frogs that invaded the garden as well as a low level `letter box` for the convenience of the postman!

The actual move itself did not go like clockwork. As usual when there was a big job on, Phil was working away from home! Packing up seven rooms to squeeze them into four was never going to be fun. It took weeks to prepare and I began to have concerns that I was doing the wrong thing. I was sobbing the day we were finished packing and wished I could retract the whole thing but it was too far down the line. People were moving into our old home the day we left and I could not go back on my word at this late stage. We were leaving a perfect house with beautiful views, lovely big rooms and colour schemes, beautiful decorative cornice, new bathroom with its huge tiles in Mediterranean green, superb fitted kitchen, shower room to go to this tiny house which needed scrubbing before we could enter it.

In exchange we had a broken down ancient cottage with half the space and in need of huge amounts of work. It had an ancient water pump, stream, and what we thought was a safe environment for cats and, joy of joys, space for the ferals! To cheer myself up and remind myself why we were making this life change we booked out the ferals from Cats Protection. Our first job lined up for the workmen was to build a huge wire mesh run with pine tree up the middle and attached to a big heated shed with heated beds inside – they had never had it so good. They were better off than us by far!

The cottage floors throughout were stone slabs, most fashionable and sought after, so we were told! I had envisaged throwing down our lovely Turkish rugs over them. Less fun was to discover that the experts advised us that to get rid of the damp we had to lift the whole floor throughout and have all that sopping wet earth dug out. We diverted the removal van and instead of moving in we spent a few hundred pounds having our belongings stored – giving us a week in which to have the place made damp free. I was most impressed by the firm who did the job – I had no time to photograph the work in progress but I well remember arriving home to find every slab had been lifted and numbered and was now sitting outside the cottage leaning against the thick walls. Inside walls had been brought down and we now had one open plan room with only the doorways and a few bits of wood panelling in place. Now that it was empty we could see rotten wood and wood a few feet up the wall and doors riddled with woodworm. The men were busy digging out piles of damp earth. Our broken down cottage was now in bits!

Edith

Our nearest neighbour - apart from the farmer - lived in one of a row of cottages about half a mile down the main road. Edith and Jim were the local Cats Protection. One evening we were there before the move when they drove down our little road and introduced themselves – they were looking for one of the cats who had escaped and been left behind when the previous owners had left. They were to catch him and have him crated and flown to the Orkneys to his new home.

Edith was a dear warm person whom I instantly befriended and she was to save me as time went on and I became more and more adversely affected by country life!

As I surveyed the mess we had bought I shuddered and took myself off to Edith`s for some comfort. Always a coffee and broad shoulder to cry on there, thank the good Lord for Edith! She was so kind and someone to whom I will always be grateful.

Once the floors were re-laid it was just a matter of renewing the walls! At least we had a good team in place to put it all together again! Our workmen were really great guys! Fred and Frank – welder and electrician – just what we needed for the feral run. Gordon the joiner who had done some lovely work for us in Newport drove all the way out to the sticks every day to help get the place habitable. What a help they all were - they really made a difference and it began to take shape slowly.

We sourced an old stained glass window which we had built into the wall between the hallway and the kitchen, a new Magnet Shaker cream kitchen to match the ancient cream Aga which of course was yet another saga as we had been told it had serviced eleven radiators so were unprepared for Douglas` our heating engineer`s verdict that it didn`t work for the seven radiators we brought him in to install.

We then had to source a suitable boiler and I don`t know why it took so long but we had a winter with no background heat - only a coal fire which was totally inadequate – and even the cats huddled together for warmth

The day we moved in the seven cats and Tabitha tortoise, I had built a wooden structure to keep Tabitha contained. Once the removal men left I noticed Tabitha was missing and went off searching for her but to no avail – she was nowhere to be seen. The garden was vast and open enough for her to escape. Tortoise can move incredibly fast when they take a notion to do so and by now she could be anywhere. This tortoise was spoiled and fed on lettuce from Marks and Spencer. We were very upset as we had loved her for many years and her loss was devastating.

However we had the eight cats to settle in and that proved easy as pie. We then had Tiggy, Kissu, Poppy, Gnasher, Ben, Sweet William, Nelson and our lovely old man Ollie! His full name was James Oliver and he had come to us on our wedding anniversary – a call from Jim Wilson of Parkside vets who knew I helped cats called to ask if I would take in this old man who had been found lying frozen into the snow by SSPCA. He had been treated and was recovering but he was very old and needed an understanding foster home. So we called him James after Jim the vet and Oliver as when we first fed him he had his first course then asked politely for more! And so Ollie joined our family – a real old gentleman who had impeccable manners stepping back to allow our resident cats to eat before him and then coming forward for his food always enjoying a two course meal of his cat food followed by a bowl of chicken!

All but Sweet William and Nelson who had escaped at the moment we needed to ship them had spent a week in a boarding cattery until the floors were re-laid. The cattery was within earshot of the kennels housing dogs, which barked incessantly. Our cats were not sorry to leave the barking dogs behind. They had an interesting time exploring their new home! The two escapees were pleased to see the rest of the feline family join us and they had a happy reunion indoors. Big bold Gnasher was first out the door to explore the new territory.

The first night in the new house was very unsettling – the security light above the large barn kept going on and off. It was quite a bit away from the house so I watched for a while and soon realised the bats were at play! I was comforted it was only bats and not a murderer on the loose!

One of the lovely things about being in the country was the ability to see the stars – we could look up to the heavens and admire thousands of stars – a sight you cannot see in the towns with street lighting interfering with the effect! It was a most dramatic atmosphere in the pitch black with only the noise of owls and night creatures going about their business! I loved the idea of the solitude. In time being alone there on the blackest of nights was exhilarating.

Once Fred had built their new enclosure we brought the five feral cats out from the shelter and loved watching them enjoy more freedom than they had had for over twelve long months. In time it was my plan to release them but at least we had given them a comfortable home in the meantime.

To celebrate the move and expand the animal family we bought a rabbit whom we called Donald and a friend for him, Angus. Donald was very large, wild and uncuddlesome Black Rex, Angus was a white black and tan guinea pig who squeaked and nibbled away at his food. They were best of friends. Phil had to start somewhere laying out the garden and decided to begin in front of their run. It would take years to lay out the beautiful garden he had in mind. There was quite an expanse of grass for cutting and I was pleased when one of my friends whose husband was a gardener came out and spent a whole day reducing the grass to ground level but we were going to have to invest in a sit on mower if we stayed any length of time!

I took time to choose décor for the house –I really enjoyed choosing the lovely colours and fabrics. There was a lot of wood panelling – even after the renewal of interior walls – and to lighten it I had it stained with a white wood stain which looked more in keeping with its age than white paint. We booked a builder to come and build an extension – a sun room the length of the house and looked forward to bringing our dining room furniture into the house and out of the barn where we now had it stored. Unfortunately before we got it indoors all our lovely stuff was ruined with rainfall. Water damaged table, chairs, as well as many boxes of books all grew mouldy by the time we got them inside.

Our First Dog

We moved in August and by September I was in battle with the neighbouring farmer whose land adjoined ours. He wanted to build a house in his field but to make things easy for him wanted to use our road as access for his lorries carrying the building materials. As this would literally be a few feet from our front door I refused on the grounds I was there to save animals and the noise and hassle of Lorries passing up and down was not conducive to a peaceful life for the animals or us!

He tried to bully me to get permission. I had visited him and his wife with a bottle of wine – as a new neighbour I did not want to start on a bad note – but ended up going to a council meeting to put my case forward. We won and I did not have to allow him access! Bearing no grudges he invited us to his end of season party, a hooley for his workers and a big barbecue in the barn. I refused the steaks on offer telling him I had spoken to the animal the previous day!

The farmer's wife ran a pheasant farm, another reason we would never be best buddies. The smell wafted over to us and I hated it when I witnessed the birds being packed into crates by net. Farm life would never impress me!

Edith was different, a lovely lady with a huge dose of compassion and a great animal lover, entirely my cup of tea. One day in September she phoned me and informed me that she had just rehomed a poodle.

"A poodle?" I repeated, thinking to myself that if there was one dog that might fit in with the cats it would be a poodle!

The poodle had gone to a lady in a nearby village but, would you believe it, she returned the poodle next day saying her son though her too old for a dog. She was 64!

Phil and I were round to Edith's like a shot to see a mad little black dog was charging up and down the small hallway like a tornado!

Happy to be back where she was wanted we saw her joyful nature and fell in love with her on sight!

Lucy came with a sad little letter. She had been the victim of a marriage break up and the man had kept her to spite his wife. Lucy was ten years old and abused – locked in a room for the past two years without love or much else. The story was that her overgrown wool and lack of walking had fused her legs together and she had been deemed incontinent and thrown on to the streets. She had been found by someone who knew Edith as a good rescuer and had led her to safety. Her pads were soft as a baby's skin and her teeth orange with rot.

Edith had given her a rough trim and filled a big bag with her wool – underneath she was a skinny girl and we looked forward to feeding and loving her! If ever a dog was like a cat it was Lucy. When we picked her up and turned her in to cuddle us she positively purred. It was so catlike that we knick named her Lucypussy.

We took her home and to introduce her to the cats put her into a huge wire meshed crate to allow the cats to see her without contact. After a few sniffs and little interest shown we let her out and she trotted into the house and sat down as if she had lived there forever. No cat had complained at all! We went about our work when all of a sudden there was a squealing and meowing and the telephone from next to our bed came flying through the air into the lounge where I was sitting! At that very moment Phil put his head round from outside saying `there`s a duck at the door`!

Talk about a madhouse - I realised the dog had jumped up on the bed where five cats lay, scattering them and causing chaos!! We couldn`t move for laughing – the animal family was growing fast and providing endless fun!

The dog fitted into our life so easily – she was so very happy to be loved and to walk. I never used to walk other than to the car. Now we had the huge forest on our doorstep and no traffic to contend with, so easy to take them all walking. The cats started off with us and some walked just a short way, others walked miles. The forest was divided into sections and I soon gave names to the various paths - Christmas Tree Lane, Fairy Toadstool Avenue, etc and Lucy just loved life with us.

She had been to the vet and the groomer. Her dental check saw her left with very few teeth and she looked skinnier than ever once her coat was cut. Her little pads were soon hardening up with the amount of walking we did – after maybe four miles I would say `shall we go home Lucy` and she would look up pleadingly to do a few more miles. She was good for us and we became fitter physically! The mental decline had not yet started.

Cat rescue

The five ferals were by this time thoroughly enjoying their extra space and one was practically human. Skippy – a big white boy with black patches and loved rolling about on his back and let us stroke him. I decided to give him his freedom and join our house cats if he so desired. I released him one Saturday as we would have the whole weekend to introduce him properly to the others. He went off to explore and I never saw him again. Despite an extensive search for weeks he was never found. I was heartbroken once more – was anything good ever going to happen here?

Now whilst all this was going on there were many local cats in need of help. One poor stray boy we called Tommy had been left with an open wound round his neck caused by a collar which had become loose. He had tried to rectify his ordeal and put his paw through the collar and managed to get his leg stuck allowing the offending collar to grow into his underarm. Poor boy had been found by a kind cat lover in Forfar, the nearest town. She had called the SSPCA who said they would come out but a day passed and no sign of them. She had heard of me and I was there like a shot to pick up the poor soul. I smelt him before seeing him and took him for immediate vet attention. It took months of healing and he stayed with us until he recovered. We got him a home in an Angus village with a loving family who adored him for the rest of his life.

Although I had wanted to help more animals than when we lived in civilisation I seemed to spend much of my time driving as distances were far greater. Even to get the morning paper was a ten mile drive as we were five miles from the nearest shop!

We had a constant stream of cats through our hands - some homed more quickly than others and one older boy we could not home at all. I called him JF (Jobby Factory) as he ate and pooed all day long, our vet assistant told us he had lived with an old man in a caravan in Tentsmuir Forest but unfortunately his old man had died. We had a caravan and I was happy to relinquish our viewing point for the deer as we never had time to wait for one or more to come along. So JF had his own home and mail arrived regularly for Mr J F Cat, The Caravan, Montreathmont Cottage, Montreathmont Moor.

It turned out he had hyperactive thyroid so was put on to daily medication. Lucy used to trot along beside me wherever I roamed and one day accompanied me to the caravan. JF had been watching at the window and when I opened his door flew out and onto Lucy's back clawing and screaming at her. I got a horrible shock and Lucy was yelping but ended up relatively unscathed with just a scratch or two. We never let her near him again and shortly after that incident he died and I suspect a brain tumour.

<u>The extension</u>

It was winter by the time the builders started our house extension. Snow was covering the ground – only a small part of which Phil had been able to lay out and tame. His plans for the Japanese garden were on hold until the better weather. All the animals were fine but it was hard work carrying the water every day for the geese. They were now confined to the big paddock to try to get our grass park into order without wading through goose dirt – not pleasant to plod through all the dirt!

We had a friend bring us two ducks along with their accommodation – Alex and Sandy – but sadly they were wild and I could not get them into their house at nights and after only three weeks they were both taken by Mr Fox.

The ducks on the huge pond belonging to the farmer were worse off. The farmer let the shooting rights to Italians who came to hunt them.

I was most unhappy about this, especially when a pellet hit the ten year old son of my joiner. As well as the pellets pinging off our front door some of the ducks fell in our garden. The countryside is not nearly as peaceful as it looks, to me it was beginning to look violent and murderous!! Numerous dead bodies on the road - mainly birds – lots of pheasant and one or two gulls but the occasional stoat, badger or fox

Let Down by the Vet

As soon as we had moved I went into the local vet and registered all our animals. Old Ollie had to have a monthly steroid injection to keep him going and I told them this and asked them to contact our Newport vet for details. I was totally unprepared for what happened therefore when I took Ollie in for his monthly jab.

I have always trusted our vet and had never any cause not to. A gung ho young man called Richard cheerfully called out `Ollie Flanders` and in we went to his surgery. He said he would give him an intravenous jab which was quite painful and why I let him go ahead with this I don`t know but I will never forgive myself for allowing him to proceed. Lambs to the slaughter!

By the time we got back home nine miles up the road old Ollie was not good. He had been fine before the jab and I could only assume that whatever the vet had given him disagreed with him and had made him ill – not long afterwards this dearest and most gentle of cats fitted and died. I will never come to terms with his death which was most untimely and very hard to bear. We later spoke to the head vet of the practice who told me they would not bill me for the treatment which had obviously killed my beloved cat. I cared not a jot about a bill – all I cared about was that Ollie was gone and it only served to prove that the wrong meds had been administered. I refused to have that vet ever again.

By now I was beginning to wish we had never moved. I was that square peg in a round hole – a very deep hole. Losing Ollie was hard. Because he had come to us in such a dreadful state in the winter of his life I was especially sad – we loved him passionately and I felt I had let him down and was responsible for losing his life. I will never forget that lovely gentle natured pussy cat who enhanced all our lives and will be forever sad when I think of James Oliver Flanders. I carry him in my heart forever.

Misery of cold weather

The winter days were hard to bear. In our old house we had central heating plus a big open fire for the coldest days. All we had now in this freezing little cottage was a small coal fire and the useless radiators we had installed and linked up to the oil fired AGA. One morning I walked into the kitchen in bare feet to find myself wading through cold sludgy slippery oil which had poured out of the Aga making life even more miserable than it already was in that godforsaken place. On top of everything else Tabitha was still missing and I had all but given up finding her by now.

The local heating engineer knew the way to us before I offered him directions – I had the feeling he knew this Aga well – he brought his nine year old son with him and together they dismantled and put it back together again! One flood cleared up but another to go! Our builder went off home one day having left a tap running – overflowing into the kitchen and from there on into the lounge I arrived home from work hours later to find our Turkish rugs floating gently through the hallway. In the midst of winter, snow on the ground and a freezing cold house with a shallow paddling pool – I did the only thing I could do and broke down and cried!!

The extension was finished in time for Christmas. It did look pretty – a large glass room with our big table at last brought in from the big barn and I went off to the local antique shop to see what I could add to the new room. The shop was down in Forfar and the owner was a lovely man called Ally who was genuinely interested in people. I told him we had bought the cottage up in the forest and we had a fine chat – it felt good to find a friend. His shop contained lots of lovely things and I admired a lovely Chesterfield sofa in its original velvet fabric – I liked it but it was a bit pricey and I left it for another day.

I did buy a really nice old pine dresser and one or two smaller pieces to enhance the house! Now the glass room was finished we put up a big Christmas tree covered in fairy lights and it looked really cosy and welcoming coming into view as we walked down the forest lane. It was January before we got the new boiler installed and life was slightly more pleasant. We had bought halogen heaters which had helped but it felt good to have central heating once more! Winter passed slowly and very cold weather added to the misery.

My lack of luxury wore me down badly and I became more depressed every day. I had lived half a mile from the library which I ran in Newport and used to be home in five minutes. I loved my job. I knew all the members like they were family and saw their children from before birth up to ending primary school. It was an extremely sociable library. No hushed silences but cheerful chatter and knowing their reading tastes I kept everyone supplied with the books they liked. I had no desire to move to a big library where I would be anonymous and knew no one. I had desperately wanted this venture to work but I was finding the country was not nearly as friendly as I had hoped. I had imagined the postman would drive up and drop in for a quick cup of coffee but he was such a grumpy man who flung our mail under the gap in the door, no happy chats there then! Even to drive home to the cottage took three quarters of an hour.

It seemed to be winter forever and as I finished work at night time I drove home over my beloved Tay Bridge, through two towns, along the motorway then up the tree lined roads with the moon shining above me lighting up my way. I had to drop into Edith to pick up Lucy then back up the dark road and down the lane to the house. It was fairly lonely arriving home to an empty cottage in the cold and running round feeding the ferals, the resident cats, any fosters, Donald and Angus. The animals saved me – it was lovely to see them enjoy the space and freedom. One day however Nelson became stuck up a high tree. With a ladder against the tree I climbed as high as I could holding some smelly raw fish. As he crawled down the branches towards me I held on to the tree with my left hand, grabbed Nelson with my right and swung him onto my chest where he clung until we got down to the ground! Phew – talk about cat rescue!!

Dog rescuer

One spring day we were walking up the forest path, Lucy and a few of the cats. Sweet William and Ben were with us about a quarter mile from the house when Lucy jumped over the ditch which ran alongside the path and I followed her over. I could hardly believe my eyes. There is front of us was Tabitha Tortoise! Eight months to the day we moved and the day she went missing. I yelled out to the cats "Look who Lucy has found!" and picked her up and ran back home, Lucy at my heels knowing she had done well. I put Tabitha in the middle of a big earth patch and Lucy dug a moat round her whilst I phoned the good news to Phil. At last something had gone right, things were looking up but not for long! When the tiles fell off the roof I knew Granny Todd was up to her mischief and decided I could no longer stay in this place.

Yet another blow was to befall us though. Our darling beautiful silver tabby boy Nelson was killed on the road at the top of our drive. All that enormous forest and he had to go the wrong way and lose his life. I carried his beautiful body down the lane and we buried him in the garden where he had spent so many happy days with the others. Once again I thought my heart would break. Another one beloved cat gone. So much for the safety of the countryside, nowhere is safe.

April 1997

The longer we were there the less I was able to do. Driving took up a good amount of time. We were too far away from home and friends for folk just to drop by and visits happened seldom as people are just too busy to travel long distances. Only Edith and Ally gave me any comfort at all. Phil was away a lot as he worked for Eurotunnel. It made such a difference when he *was* at home as the fire would be burning and the house lit up when I got home from the library at night time. Driving down our private road in the pitch black to an empty house was no fun at all.

I knew I was not going to be happy in this place after all. I was afraid to tell Phil after the huge upheaval but I could keep it to myself no longer.

His job took him to Paris every few weeks and I would sometimes accompany him on these trips. I remember being there with him in the hotel and telling him I couldn't stay and him replying "Don`t worry we're going home tomorrow." and then having to admit that I actually meant our new home.

It was out now! Unbeknown to me though he had arranged a surprise party for my birthday and when we returned home there were about fifty people at the house to welcome me home. I felt positively ill.

I was not number one in the popularity stakes as you can imagine but, being the kind man he is, he let me start putting the wheels in motion to regain my sanity and return to where I loved best! I promised him a round-the- world trip when we got back and that is what happened. My priority was to find a home for the remaining four feral cats. Luckily for them a local optician in the little town had a beautiful country estate and was willing to take the whole family and so they moved from their big heated pen with tree to a lovely stone cottage of their own adjoining the big house and lived happily ever after.

We had a queue of five prospective owners after the cottage which by now looked fabulous compared with how it was when we bought the place. We lost out financially but learned a lot. We found a house back in the village I would always think of as home. It was nothing like our lovely house but was suitably safe for the cats and well away from the spells of Granny Todd. We drove back with six cats in baskets, Gnasher had broken out of his and was hanging round my neck and Tabitha Tortoise was crawling over my feet. In those days we had to stop at the toll booth on the bridge and I could open the window only a couple of inches or Gnasher might have landed in the Tay!

Back home

Lucy still loved her walks and we adored Lucy and life revolved round her. Phil was besotted by her and to this day adores little black dogs. We took her everywhere. She was such an outgoing friendly girl and loved visiting with us and was so well behaved and a joy! We missed the forest on the doorstep but we had the beaches within easy reach and she loved life with us. At home she would jump from chair to chair around the room – not good behaviour for a big Labrador but such fun for our wee soul!

We walked miles along the huge beach at Tentsmuir and back through the forest day after day. One freezing cold winter's day we took her to East Sands at St Andrews and on to the beach she ran. She had never ventured into the water before but we had just arrived when she ran into the freezing water and just stood there! The waves were about to wash her off her feet and Phil ran in and grabbed her and we wrapped her into my fleece and headed off home. We think then she was starting to go senile. She had had kidney disease for the past six months and by now I was having to feed her by hand. The renal diet food warmed in the microwave was not too pleasant a texture and it would stick to my hand but I would do anything to prolong her life whilst it was still good quality. We knew time was running out for our little soul and wanted to keep her happy as long as possible. She was still on her feet but not eating when one Sunday in January 2001 we had to call in the vet and say goodbye to our dear little black girl. I did not know how I would be able to bear it but I got such a shock to see Phil cry for the first time ever since I knew him that I held it together for his sake. Even the vet was upset as he too had known Lucy for some long time. We had five and a half years of utter joy with this dearest little dog whom we were privileged to have had in our lives and who will forever be missed.

Sophie

I still walked down to the beach most days. People would stop me to ask after Lucy and I missed her more than anything. Cats are pets and I love ours with a passion, but a dog is a way of life. I decided I would get another poodle and started looking for a rescue. Being totally against breeding of cats and dogs due to the world over population I looked to the local rescues but could not locate a poodle. I was glad in a way that no poodles were in need. However my friend Lindsey, who is nurse at the local vet surgery, told us of a six year old female miniature apricot in need of a home. The story was she had been given as a gift to a young widow who had not had time to do much training with her. She had taken an aversion to a foster child in her home and so she had to go, but she was in Peterborough.

When I told Phil it all fell into place as his colleague Bob was in Peterborough that week. Due to drive up to Glasgow he arranged to meet the rescue lady at a service area and bring the dog up country. It was a Friday night when Phil nipped over to Glasgow to pick up our new pet and I was waiting at home excited as never before for years. I had the chicken breast ready for her supper and probably beans for Phil. He was used to seeing the ovens full of roasting chickens and knowing they were for the feral cats!

Well when she arrived it was just lovely to bring her out of her crate and into the warm house. She ran round the lounge and we kept her apart from the cats to give her a chance to settle in without distractions. We took her up to our bedroom where she spent the night at my side of the bed and she slept well. In the morning I could hear the cats outside our bedroom door and thought I would let them meet. She had to meet them sometime. It went well and soon they were all investigating the new arrival. We introduced her to the forest next day and on the Sunday took her to the big beach where she played and then home for dinner!

On the Monday morning after our forest walk she had breakfast then lay on the beanbag in front of the fire. I knelt down to stroke her head and she bit hard right through my hand.

I was stunned – and scared – and dripping blood. It was very painful and I wondered if this was the real reason for her owner giving her up. Just our third day and the start of finding just how difficult a dog could be. I took her to the vet in case there was anything medically wrong and she did have an ear infection. I bought the muzzle they used to handle her. That was well worth the money and well used. We tried to get the eardrops into her ear by feeding her lumps of liver cake and hoped to get the drops in whilst she munched but instead she bit through Phil's thumb. We now both had a sore hand and sympathised with each other. No sweet little dog this girl, but she needed us and was here to stay.

I took her to the dog training class and she bit the trainer. I was advised to be heavy handed with her but apart from by now being afraid of her it is not my style to physically abuse a dog. I decided to go for the TLC route and from then on we learned what could and could not be done with Sophie. She was nothing like our beloved Lucy then or ever. No longer could I pick up my dog and swing her round into my arms. We learned never to touch her in her bed and had to be on our guard all the time and never have her near children.

In fact I am sure the vet would have had her put to sleep but we wanted to give her every chance and we did.

We got the offer of another poodle over the phone in 2007 and I accepted right away. Her name was Candy and she was six years old. Unfortunately she ran away before they brought her to us and I was then left disappointed and wanting another dog.

It was then I found Dog Aid Society of Scotland when I visited their website and saw the first picture of the dog that was to be our new boy. He was a neglected Bichon Frise called Cracker.

Cracker dog

Cracker was advertised on the website as fourteen year old Bichon Frise friendly boy with three legs and use of one eye. The chances of there being a queue for him were slight and I immediately offered him a home. We had a home check to pass and were deemed suitable despite our naughty dog Sophie. That was her one saving grace – she did like other dogs. We arranged to have Cracker brought to my daughter's home in Linlithgow as they were bringing him directly from his home in Edinburgh. Once again I was excited as a kid in a sweet shop and could not wait to meet him. Helen from Dog Aid brought him for that first meeting to the nearby park. As on previous first meetings I felt it best to meet on mutual territory then go home together. When we first saw Cracker he was bedraggled, filthy and the friendliest bundle of joy ever. I cried to see him in such a dreadful state but Helen pointed out he had not been ill-treated or he would not have been so friendly. However I was none too sure as Lucy too had been a bright spark when we met and she had been abused.

We adored him from the start. We took him home and threw out the scabby collar and lead and got him into the shower. The dirt just floated down the drain and left him with bright pink skin below his now bright white tangled coat which had definitely seen better days!

I had him booked into our groomer but she could not take him right away and so he had a clean but matted coat in which to go on holiday. We were just about to leave for our Scottish Highland holiday complete with dogs.

As we were packing the car I noticed Cracker was no longer in the house! He was walking on his three legs up the middle of the main road where we live and coming down was a big jeep. I went screaming out, hands waving to stop it and scooped up the dog who wondered what all the fuss was about. Cracker had arrived and the fun began!

We had a great holiday with the pair of them. They got on well with each other and with other dogs. They was no problem when we went out for a meal and the pair of them stayed happily and peacefully together whilst we ate out. Back home Cracker soon made friends with the daily dog walking crowd and became well known for running sideways on his three legs barking and growling then jumping up onto the big dogs. This was his idea of fun! Everyone adored him and we were glad to have a friendly pet again. He was with us for two years and a month. One day, a month before he died, he seemed to go off the legs. It was a Saturday night and out of hours for our vet. I rushed him over to St Andrews surgery, carried him into the surgery and put him down. He walked round the room. I paid the £170 bill a bit grudgingly but was very happy that he was still with us.

A month later one Sunday in the forest he went down again and this time could no longer walk. I carried him home and fed him all his favourite treats whilst we awaited the vet. It was Will, the same vet that had come to put Lucy down.

Sophie stood at the back of the room whilst her friend went gently to sleep and we were yet again sobbing into our Kleenex!

Over the nine and a half years we had Sophie she was never an easy dog. Her last New Year aged 16 she was sitting between us on the sofa and when we kissed at midnight she decided to bite Phil as he put his hand forward, and so we started the New Year dripping blood once more! She proved that no matter how well she was treated or how long she stayed her biting never left her.

We missed Cracker very much and I started to look for another dog. I liked having two to watch run through the forest together. This time a toy poodle boy turned up from the Many Tears rescue. Jack had spent seven long years at a puppy farm being used for breeding. He was now in a foster home in Edinburgh. That clinched it as he had was just an hour away. I spoke to the fosterer, Joyce Wishart, and discovered we knew quite a number of animal people in common. After a recommendation from our vet we arranged to take Sophie along to meet Jack in an Edinburgh car park. I couldn't wait!

We introduced the pair outside and had a little walk together then Phil cuddled the little boy as I drove home. He was a timid little creature and I was appalled when we got to the forest as it was obvious he had not been walked and he really had no clue as to sniffing or doing doggy things at all. He just stared up at me and I felt sorry for the little soul. He did not seem to like Phil at all which was a bit unfair knowing his loving of poodles. However in time and with Phil`s patience almost four years later they have grown quite close.

Sophie died in 2012 aged sixteen and a half. The end of an era. We had her nine and a half years.

Facebook

In 2011 I became very involved in animal rescue abroad via Facebook. I was previously aware of the cruelty to animals in Eastern Europe but nothing prepared me for some of the appalling and dreadful sights to be seen on Facebook. I was shocked and sickened and vowed to help where I could. This was manifested mainly in handing over vast amounts of money to rescuers and hoping they were legitimate.

The first cat I saw in a filthy state that I tried to help was Gupta. To truly rescue any of the animals we see we must offer to foster or adopt. Realistically, being two thousand or more miles away from them, fostering in Scotland is hardly an option. By the time we pay the fare to get them here we really want to keep them ourselves. To offer a home is literally to save the life of the animal, as left in some of these countries is a death sentence for most. I pledged to bring Gupta to Scotland and the rescuer took him off the streets and into the vet. However this poor cat was too far gone and despite being treated in an incubator he died. They did their best but this dear suffering soul was never going to make it to Scotland. It is like being with a family on Facebook of like minded people and we had a candle lit vigil for him. I was bereft and sat and sobbed for him and all the others who were at the mercy of some extremely cruel people.

The dogs gave even more concern. Thousands of street dogs at risk of being caught by the professional dog catchers, who are mainly thugs being paid a lot of money to pick up dogs from the streets and, quite literal throw them into public shelters. If you think the dog pound back in UK is not pleasant it is a great deal better than the conditions these dogs have to endure for varying periods from weeks to many years. Miserable and hopeless many give up the will to live.

The next cat we offered to rehome was Tufftom. He was an older street cat who had been blinded by acid. He reminded me in looks of our Sweet William and I had no hesitation in offering him our home. In the meantime a young woman rescuer Emma Sayuri had posted on Facebook a white and ginger cat she called Moonlight. He too needed a home. He had appeared out of the blue as she fed her street cats in the dark. He was thin as a rake. He had practically jumped into her arms and so she took him home to her flat known as Kitty Kindergarten!

Well he could never have known then the lovely future he would have as we chose him out of the hundreds looking for homes. He was to be the eyes for Tufftom – or so I thought until Tufftom also died before he left the vet. Another heartache but this time his fare was paid and I did not want to lose the place on the transport. I asked Emma which cat had a passport and was ready to travel as we had a very short time to arrange a replacement and the only one was a six month old kitten called Annabelle!

I really did not want a young cat – being older myself a kitten was not an attractive proposition. I imagined her climbing the curtains and causing havoc – nonsense I could live without. However better take her and use the space which cost over four hundred pounds. The advantage was that she and Moonlight knew each other well and would be company for each other on the long journey.

I had also fallen in love with a puppy from the Bucharest streets who also needed a home. His rescuer called him Michael and he too was booked to travel. They were all coming to us on 29 September 2012.

The day arrived and I was excited beyond words. The two pussies we put upstairs into the cat room to settle down and recover from their marathon journey of six days. They went into the corner of the room and Annabelle sat on top of Moonlight gazing at us. Phil sat on the floor speaking to them and within minutes they were over to investigate their first encounter with a Scotsman! They never looked back and they are now firmly established over two years on and loved beyond words. Adorable pussies who lie in each others arms still and are full of love for us and the other pets, cats and dogs in this madhouse.

Puppy Michael was a delight and a joy from the minute he arrived. Everyone loves Michael. He has shown no behavioural problems at all and despite being found and rescued from the Bucharest streets at four months old is the most laid back and happiest of dogs.

I was becoming a bit afraid to invite another cat to join us as we had yet another disappointment. A gentle tabby girl had met some lowlife in Timisoara who had cut off her ear. Her name was Scarlet and I loved her too on sight. Another case of spending months in a cage at the vet then came home to her rescuer Sonia Neamt one weekend. She passed away in Sonia`s arms and once again we were left with a sore heart and longing for this little soul who would never make the journey.

The pain these rescuers have to endure is endless. They see daily sights that would make any animal lover cringe. They are compelled to help injured and paralysed animals all the time. The Romanian public do not believe in neutering but instead allow their dogs and cats to breed indiscriminately and then dump the puppies or kittens in forests or even by the roadsides. The roads are therefore strewn with dead dogs and cats and I would never be able to visit the country of birth of six of our current pets.

Our cat family now includes Jojo a tiny tabby and white girl who came to us from a dog shelter in Valcea where she was born and lived for six years before coming to UK. She is the tiniest cat we have ever owned and is also the clumsiest. She has so far broken three lamps by hauling them over, our marble fireplace by knocking a flower vase on to the hearth. The vase did not even crack but the marble tile was left chipped. The latest breakage is the middle tile in my kitchen. She managed to knock the iron from the worktop on to the floor leaving an iron-shaped indent in the huge tile. She has certainly made her mark but for all that we adore her totally.

Motanski cat came from Constanta. A ginger boy with missing back paw he now lives the high life with us after a few years of cold unwelcoming street life. He loves all the cats here and has no fear of our dogs. He loves nothing better than climbing up high and surveying his garden territory. He is playful indoors and plays with all the cat toys. Jojo goes to the toy container and paw picks out toys for play.

I shall now have to become blinkered where it comes to rehoming as we are at our limit. Our latest dog was found in the Romanian snow covered mountains in a dreadful state. He had been bitten by dogs and beaten by humans and was covered in thistles and starving. Goodness knows how long he had been struggling but was lucky to be found and taken to a wonderful lady who rescues dogs in Braila.

Sofia Gabriela Catruna took this dog into her home. I was attracted by his story and felt we could cope with this little boy. Bubu has been with us for eight months now. He has his worries – is terrified of strange dogs, scared of strange people, scared of anything strange to him. He is hyperactive first thing in the mornings, barks his head off when in the car but he also has his good points. He is very loving and likes nothing better than sitting on my lap facing in with paws round my neck. Twice now he has even kissed me. He is great with the cats and now interacts with Jack and Michael and now has started to play with the dogs in the forest we meet every day. They say you don`t always get the dog you want but the dog you need. Bubu is certainly a learning process but whether or not we need him makes me wonder at times. We might find out the answer to that another day.

The Life of Flash

By

Ian Stewart

Ian Stewart left school in 1977 with no qualifications. Later in life he decided to become a mature student and first acquired a photographic qualification. After this he graduated from the University of Sheffield with a BA Hons. in Social History and Geography. A variety of jobs, mostly within the education sector, followed. Today he is semi-retired and a full-time dog walker.

Ian is a first time writer who has chosen to write about the life and times of his beloved dog Flash.

The Beginning

My previous dog had passed away on Halloween 1995, Sandy was sixteen years old, a good age. My mother had died in November of the previous year and Sandy had never really been the same since then. Regardless of all this we made a decision to get another dog. We eventually went to Allerton Bywater, near Castleford in West Yorkshire to a place called Ponderosa Kennels. They had just had a litter of pups in that were six weeks old and there were three of them left. Two of them were black and with a curly type of coat. These two came towards us and greeted us when we entered into their enclosure. The third one was a lot quieter and stayed at the back of the enclosure. It was a dog and had a smooth beige/sandy coat. With a white flash on his head and with four white socks on each leg, he was our obvious choice. However, he was still too young and was waiting for his final injections. We went back the following week and he was promptly put in a small box for us to take away. He cost us the princely sum of £70.00. He didn't made a sound as he left the kennels and he never stirred on the first leg of our bus journey home.

We decided to go into a café for some fish and chips in Castleford and while we were there he popped his head out of the box. The waitress smiled and commented, "Ah isn't he cute". This would not be the last time someone said that about him.

We caught the train for the next stage of our journey and made sure he didn't pop his head out again - we weren't going to pay a fare for such a small creature, we could have put him in our pocket if we'd have wanted to! He never made any attempt to get out of the box and we completed a last leg on the bus without incident.

From being a quiet little thing he soon found his bearings and was a tiny terror. He went for things be it human, canine or feline but only because he wanted to lick, bite or chase them respectively. He was into everything and found his way out of the back garden through any tiny hole even if it looked like a mouse couldn't get through it. My neighbour brought him back round on more than one occasion. We eventually filled in the holes in the fence and made the garden secure, but he was cute and most of the local kids thought so. Groups of girls would stop us in the street and want to stroke him, something he wasn't too keen on. Eventually as Flash grew older most of them were wary of him but that wasn't a bad thing in our eyes, not having children of our own.

One night near Christmas time someone tried to break into the house. They didn't succeed in getting in, but they did succeed in damaging the back window and the patio door. While waiting for these to be repaired we ended up not being able to open the back patio door and had to use the front door. The front door led out into an open garden that was not suitable for a puppy to be let out into on its own. We had to take Flash down the passage on a lead and direct it to the back garden. This scenario kept up into the New Year partly because the weather was too bad for the workmen to come out and what with their backlog of work it would be well into February before we had the repairs done. In the meantime in late January my father caught pneumonia and was gravely ill. We already knew what the doctor would confirm, that he was dying. The only thing to be decided was to take him in hospital or to leave him peacefully in his bed. We decided on the latter option and he passed away very peacefully on January 30th 1996. The funeral was organised for the following Monday and we still did not have a back door. There weren't that many people due to come back to the house but some of them were elderly and infirm. Flash, being the puppy he was, liked to run around like a little nutter. This didn't go down too well with some of the family and friends who came back after the funeral. With this in mind we decided to put Flash into the spare room and close the door on him, obviously, we looked in on him from time to time. The first couple of times he was fine. We expected to find a little puddle maybe but he had been fairly good with this and was largely house trained. However, the third time we looked in on him we found that he had started to tear a cardboard box up, so down he came. The next thing we knew one of my old aunties was wailing that the little devil was biting her ankles. He went on a lead but he caused a laugh and made the atmosphere a lot lighter.

Both of us were working at this time and Flash was left sometimes far longer than he should have been. On the whole though, he was pretty good and we only came home once to find he'd been "a bad 'un". He had gnawed two of the table legs and a couple of chairs. We still have these so they weren't damaged too much! One time Brian came home from work and put a chicken salad sandwich on the side. He was distracted for a time doing something else and when he returned to the kitchen there was a breadcake and some lettuce and tomato on the floor but no sign of any chicken! Flash got shouted at for this apparently. I found the whole episode quite amusing when I came home later.

For some reason we were never to find out, Flash didn't like other dogs. He'd run off if he was off the lead or he took a lunge at them and bit their nose end. Keeping a constant look out for other dogs and putting him on the lead easily rectified the first thing. The second wasn't too bad providing the other dog's owner put them on their lead but this didn't always happen. We had to apologise profusely to one dog owner as Flash bit her dog and drew blood on its nose, the dog yelped a lot! We had to be careful and try and pick our walks to suit Flash for all his long life.

We used to have the milk delivered, a practice that went out a long time ago because of the cost. After about six months Flash had become a great guard dog. Any knock at the door would be greeted by loud barks and the milkman was terrified of him. This was something we encouraged after our recent attempted burglary. One day though Flash was rumbled, although not by the milkman. We answered the door to someone and Flash sped out straight past the startled man on the doorstep. Across the car park from us there lived a white cat and Flash had seen it. He chased it up the passage around the back of the houses opposite. Before we had time to run after him he was racing back with the white cat in hot pursuit. We laughed and laughed but we took some time catching him again. A couple of times he ran up to the road where we live. Admittedly it is only a quiet cul-de-sac traffic wise but cars have had to suddenly stop for him and this would set a scenario that would come back to haunt us at a later date in his life.

Walks and Everyday Life

Flash's early walks were mostly local for a variety of reasons. We were both working, we didn't have a car and of course he didn't want to go too far whilst he was still a puppy. The most local of local walks was around the "lump", along the main road on a lead and then around the back of the old people's home and off the lead on the adjacent grass. Near where we live was a car park used only by a few workers at the steel works. At the far end of this were some huts used by the garden club. When they weren't in attendance this was a large open space fenced off on three sides. This was ideal for teaching Flash to come back and sit, etc, while getting him used to fetching balls and the like.

Two of his first walks were to the "little woods" and the "big woods". The former went round the back of some houses and we could encounter dogs on a certain section so Flash went on the lead here. The latter was officially called Oxley Park in Stocksbridge. This was a very popular place for all types of dog walkers. We learnt to go at certain times to avoid certain people and their dogs. Nevertheless, Flash was chased a few times at this place and eventually we stopped going. Another local place good for Flash was the cemetery. Not around the graves, although some people did go there with their dogs. We went at the top end that was more like a park than a cemetery. This was a great place to take the ball and let Flash lose some of his excess energy without encountering other dogs and without ourselves expelling too much energy.

As Flash got older we took him further afield on the local buses. He never liked the noisy, older buses that Stocksbridge had and still has on its routes. Some of the more pleasant bus drivers got to know him and some always refused a fare for him.

One of the main places for a walk was Underbank Dam. This walk could be extended by walking both ways or catching a bus to Midhopestones or Langsett and walking back. Alternatively you could go to Langsett and walk around there and catch the bus back a couple of hours later. In the better weather we would do this on a regular basis. It involved a circular walk or going off the beaten track and going on an irregular route. This was better for not seeing other dogs but sometimes entailed spooking the occasional deer out of its lair. We quickly learnt the better paths and got to know just about every route in the place. By catching the same timed bus you saw other people who did the same every day. There was one old guy who always grumbled about Flash moaning but he also grumbled about just about everything else as well so no one took any notice of him. These walks were favourites of ours and I would meet Brian on the bus sometimes straight from work or college or university depending on where I was coming from at the time and at what stage of my life I was at. We've even taken him on a walk when I had bags of books brought home with me to study. The main drawback was whether or not the bus would turn up for our return. Many a time we would be waiting a couple of hours or we decided to walk all the way back rather than wait. We didn't wait at the bus stop but we'd go and waste some time on another part of the walk we'd done previously.

By changing buses at the Flouch roundabout one could get down to parts of the old Woodhead railway line. Indeed many other sections could be explored by staying on the bus towards Penistone. Many people commented to us that Flash could have been a gun dog and he proved it to us here once when walking past a local clay pigeon shoot, he never flinched when the guns were going off all around him.

Another bus took us up to Bolsterstone where a great walk took us up the hill to the beacon. This went past some sheep. We were always wary of Flash with sheep, on more than one occasion he had chased some before coming back to be scolded. Walking up to the beacon started on a minor lane, you had to be watching for traffic but not too alertly. On this one occasion we were doing this instead of watching for sheep. Flash went through an opening in a gate and the next thing we knew about fifty sheep were neatly rounded up in one corner of the field. The little devil came running back all pleased with himself.

A few local places were really not suitable for a dog that could find mud where others couldn't. Wharncliffe Crags, Sheephouse Woods and the path around Tin Mill fell into this category and you could count the number of times Flash went to these places probably on one hand. Another place was at Deepcar and entailed walking across the metal railway bridge that had numerous gaps in it, not for the faint hearted!

When Flash got a bit older, (about seven I would guess), we discovered Bramall Lane situated at the back of the steelworks. This place was a revelation, a long path with no road to intrude on it. This was ideal to let Flash off the lead for a long walk without constantly looking around for vehicles. For around the last ten years of his life it was his and our preferred walk. We got to know the other dog walkers who on the whole were a decent bunch and when he got older would ask us in the street or on at the shops how he was doing if they hadn't seen him for a while. Even today most people in Stocksbridge don't know where it is and even more people don't know its actual name. If you mentioned it to people they normally thought you were going somewhere near the football ground in Sheffield, "That's a strange place to take the dog"!

We also followed a particular ritual on Christmas Day. While Brian was busy cooking the festive dinner I'd take Flash the full length of Bramall Lane and through the steelworks. It was eerily quiet and no one was around. By the time we got back the dinner would be almost ready and the giblets ready for Flash to consume.

We first had the use of a car on a permanent basis in 2008. By this time Flash was getting on a bit and didn't need to go as far for a walk. Brian was also suffering with arthritis and couldn't walk too far either. Nevertheless, Flash still went far and wide in the car, he just walked a bit less. Even though the car opened up a whole new world of walks for us, Flash still went on Bramall Lane more often than not. He would moan in the car if not let out fairly quickly and acquired what we called "second walk syndrome", if he wasn't let out again soon after his first walk he started to moan even more. This was especially so when we went on holidays and we had to devise even more new places to stop at on the way.

So, where to take him further afield? Luckily I knew a lot of places very well due to going walking myself in the countryside.
Reservoirs always figured highly in walks with Flash, probably due to their propensity around this area. Apart from the aforementioned Underbank, Langsett and Midhope sites, quite a few more saw Flash make his appearance over the years. Winscar was a great place on a nice day, not too far but far enough to offer us all a change of scene. Unfortunately, we'd only been going there a couple of years before Yorkshire Water decimated the place with their "works". This

seems to be a thing Yorkshire Water did on a regular basis. Anyone who has ever been to these reservoirs will know what I'm talking about. Langsett's lovely footpaths were rendered almost inaccessible for a couple of years while they completed their work there. Admittedly, they made a good job at that dam and the paths there now are more numerous than they previously were. Ewden reservoir is one of the finest walks and views to be found locally and as Flash became older still we took him down there a few times. It was relatively flat for both Flash and Brian, so suited them both nicely. After taking Flash to both Thurgoland and Ingbirchworth reservoirs both were found to be unsuitable. Nearby though is Broadstone reservoir, a little known much smaller dam. Situated near the windmills that blight the landscape around Thurlstone this is a quiet oasis where a peaceful walk can be experienced. The walk was just enough for all parties to be happy with the distance.

Rather than leave Flash sometimes when we were either going into Sheffield or Hillsborough shops, we would take him with us in the car. Wadsley Common is a great place for dog walking but not if, like Flash, you don't like other dogs. The place was far too busy and we started to take him further down the valley to Loxley, where a short walk beside the river did the trick. Glen Howe Park was another decent walk but too hilly for someone with too many ailments such as Brian. This place though was good if the weather was really hot when Flash was old, either that or we would take him in the shady woods at the top of Long Lane. When Flash needed a short walk or when the weather was most fowl Pea Royd Woods or the then recently installed millennium beacon fitted the bill. We'd pick cherries or sloes on this path but it had a few corners and we never knew what was around them. Neither did Flash and this could make him a bit on the nervous side.

Brian and myself have always liked to do a bit of shopping in Buxton and again, on occasion Flash would come with us. A stop was usually made before the Strines pub. The second stop was invariably down on the path that connects Bamford with Thornhill. Another stop both on the way there and on the way back was at Millers Dale, this was also a good stop for us humans with the toilets being very handy there. We never dragged him around Buxton though, it was far too busy for his temperament.

There were a few places that were really one-offs. Places that seemed a good idea at the time but sometimes were never repeated for reasons that sometimes escape us now. We took him for a picnic down at Hayfield once. A reasonably flat place for an older dog but pretty boring for us. Once, and just the once, we took Flash onto the top of the Woodhead. The place is called Salter's Brook after the old pack horse bridge there that was used hundreds of years ago by the men who delivered the salt over those hills. The Woodhead being the Woodhead was misty and cold in complete contrast to home where it was sunny and a rather nice day. Needless to say we were not dressed for the occasion. We hurriedly crossed the road, which is not an easy task in itself. The wind was by now bringing some rain down and rather than spend some time down in the bottom where it is rather pleasant on a nice day, we just turned round straight away and marched Flash back to the car.

One of our favourite trips out, especially on a summer Sunday was to the side of the canal at Slaithwaite. We would go to the Harry Heywood's fish and chip shop for the full works and bring them back to the canal lock. There is an island that was just right to let Flash off on and he would wait patiently for his scraps, chips and fish bits.

Some people say that dogs like a routine, most humans as well. Well Flash certainly had a daily routine for most of his early life. Both Brian and I left home early in the day and Flash was left alone. Brian was working and would come home around noon and take Flash for a small walk. We would both return at teatime and he would go his long walk.

When we first got him I was still at University and I would be gone for long days at a time. First lecture was at nine in the morning and a last one could be at four. It took me over an hour to get there from Stocksbridge. The first winter we had Flash I only took him a walk at weekends. After I graduated I found a job easily but never really enjoyed my work and the long hours. I changed jobs on a regular basis and eventually found one part-time and locally, both of which I was looking for. This made a big difference to our lives and to the life of Flash, he went far more walks.

All this changed Flash's routine enormously but he still experienced a daily routine, albeit one that changed from month to month. As the nights became lighter he went more walks and went further. He would wait patiently for his long walk all day and then was so excited when it was eventually time to go. We both looked forward all day to the time to go ourselves and our entire life evolved around Flash.

Flash liked many different things to eat. He was especially fond of pork scratchings, apple cores, cheese and chicken. I used to put pork scratchings on the settee arm and make him wait before he could have them. He would sit there patiently. While we never trained Flash, he would sit when told and would perform a variety of little tasks for tit-bits. When he was younger he had a tin of dog food a day supplemented by biscuits and tit-bits and we managed his weight quite well. He never got fat, unlike his owners! People used to comment to us that he always looked a picture of health. It wasn't until he got into his teens we actually read what it said on one of the tins of his food and noticed it said a dog of his size should have two tins a day. From then on that's what he received. He still never got fat but the extra food was consumed with gusto.

<u>Holidays</u>

Flash was just two years old when he went on his first holiday. On this, our first holiday, we stayed on a fairly quiet chalet park in Mundesley in Norfolk. Flash could come straight out of the door and wander round the grassed off park area. Five minutes took us to the cliff top, well, as much a cliff as Norfolk possesses. A path a little further on led to the beach. It was a perfect location for him. The chalet itself was a bit dirty on our arrival and we vowed to try and get somewhere a little better for ourselves next time we went away. Further up the coast the cliff did indeed get a little higher. Flash had a habit of picking up stones and even sticks on rare occasions. We always tried to get rid of these, up a tree was the favoured place, although Flash on more than one occasion actually climbed the tree to retrieve the said article. We were walking on the path above the beach one day and I kicked a stone Flash had brought us down onto the beach. Flash promptly jumped down onto the beach, a mere twenty feet or so below. Naturally he then couldn't get back up again so we had to coax him to follow us until we came to a path where he could get back up to us. One afternoon we took him on a bus to Trimingham and walked back to Mundesley on the beach. Anything to tire him out! On the way back from this holiday Flash attended his first football game. We stopped at Bourne on the Saturday afternoon. This ground is situated in a public park and we took him out for a walk at half time and at full time before we continued our journey home. He was fine staying in the car and we always made sure he was in the shade and the windows wound down. We had hired a car for the holiday and all had gone well. We looked forward to our next sojourn.

The next holiday was the following year at roughly the same time, September. We stopped at Backwell on the way down for our football fix where the car was parked under some trees to provide the necessary shade for Flash. We decided to stay in a caravan in Charmouth in Dorset. Again, a car was hired from the same company we hired one from last time. The owner offered us a better car, a large Rover, we naturally jumped at the offer. This was a massive mistake on our part, we should have known better given the reputation Rover had at the time. The big end blew just this side if Ilminster. I drove it into a quiet lane and set off to try and find a phone. Oh, for a mobile phone in those days. The first house I came to looked promising. However, just before I entered the garden through the gate I noticed that the man in the garden was naked. I decided to go to the next house. It was a little way along the lane. As I was walking there what passed me but a towing truck from a local garage. A stroke of luck. He towed us to our caravan we had booked in at. The car hire company said they would pay for the cost of being towed and would reimburse us for a hire car while we were down there. He also told us that the AA would tow the car home when we were due to return. We contacted a local car hire firm who brought the car to our caravan for us. It was an older car than the one we had had originally but it did the trick for the rest of the week. The caravan park was a small one with about eight vans perched on the actual clifftop. This was in 1998 and since then the park has disappeared in one of the many landslips that the area experiences. The walk to Lyme Regis over these cliffs was the most popular one that week. On the Tuesday we left Flash in the car park at Weymouth while we went to the game there, this was his first experience of a larger crowd and he was a little scared as they all walked passed the car on their way home.

Promptly on the Saturday morning the AA appeared. The car, with us inside it, ended its journey in the car park at the back of our house. Flash behaved impeccably on the journey home even though he had to stay in our car on his own for the whole time we were moving. The upshot of all this was that the car hire firm refused to give me any compensation and blamed me for the car breaking down. After a few months of wrangling with them I won a small claims court battle with them and I was awarded the full cost of the other hire car and £400 compensation for my inconvenience. Still the car hire firm refused to pay, so, eventually, the bailiffs were sent in and recovered the full amount as well as their own costs. Not long after this the company ceased operations, whether it had anything to do with my case is open to conjecture. This whole charade slightly put us off this type of holiday and it was May 2001 before we took Flash away again.

May 2001 saw us taking Flash to Spittal, near Berwick-on-Tweed. We went straight there this time but went on the Sunday instead of the Saturday. A small flat right on the promenade provided another perfect place for Flash. It was even lit at night and gave us the opportunity to take him out much later than he ever went at home. We took some great photographs of him here on the beach digging up the stones we had buried for him. He adored this activity and did it every time he went on a beach right into his seventeenth year. We indulged in fish and chips on the Cockburnspath beach one evening and both the food and setting were good enough for us to return a few times when we went past the place to Scotland on other holidays. This time the return journey was broken by a stay in Knaresborough on the Saturday afternoon but Flash stayed in the car for most of it.

The following September saw us going north to Scotland, a place called Ballantrae was to be our base. For this vacation we went on the Thursday, something we never repeated. It was to do with football again and we rushed up to Scotland in time to get to Kilmarnock to watch them play in the UEFA Cup. The road seemed to be long and was full of twists and turns, so much so that Flash was sick on the back seat. This was a rare event and normally he was a good traveller. Our chalet this time was on a small park that was set deep in some woods. This was superb for Flash and I think we just about went down every path there was on offer. We saw owls just about every night of our stay. Our mornings were spent at a local café where the breakfast was good and reasonably priced. The journey home was slightly less hair-raising.

One year later we went to Walton-on-the-Naze in an upstairs flat. The flat itself was adequate without being luxury. The beauty of it though was that it opened directly onto the cliff top walk. Well, again, what they pass for cliff tops in Essex anyway. Every morning, sometimes ridiculously early, Flash would go a walk on here. The Naze itself was a great place for dog walking with plenty of paths from the car park and an old, disused lighthouse as a focal point. A superb walk went round a dyke in Kirby-le-Soken and round the backwaters but Flash never went on that one, it being a bit wet in places. Indeed the second time I went it had all flooded and was under several feet of water.

Once again it was one year later before we went on our holidays again, this time to the opposite side of the country to Porlock in Somerset. The cottage was a semi-detached and just around the corner from it was a direct path to the marsh. This was a narrow path with a fence on one side and a deep edge on the other. The fence was very handy to throw stones over so that Flash couldn't get to them again. He had a habit of swallowing too many of them so we used to do this to stop him. One afternoon we had gone past the narrowest part and on to the adjacent lane. Flash picked up his customary stone. I took it off him and threw it over the tall edge. He found a way through the edge and the next minute he was at the other side. The only problem was he couldn't get back through to our side. We tried to find a gap to coax him through but to no avail. We had to retrace our steps and open a gate so he could get back. He was cursed ever so slightly. This holiday was the first when we had a bit of cash to go to the pub with. There was one at the end of our road so one night we decided to have a meal and a few pints for a change. At chucking out time I decided to take Flash down the lane to the marsh for a midnight walk. I'd had a few pints as you may have guessed. Flash was never bothered by the dark and all went well. We saw a couple of owls and loads of bats flying around the marsh at that hour.

Our new found wealth must have extended to the following year, (2004) because we took Flash on no less than three holidays that year. The first saw us venturing north to Scotland at the end of March. We stayed in a cottage right on the seafront at a place called Isle of Whithorn. We stopped at Dumfries on the way up for the football and both Brian and I were bored rigid by the game we chose, which finished in a nil-nil draw. I miscalculated the time it would take us to get to the cottage from Dumfries and it was dark well before we arrived at our property for the week. To make matters worse there was a detour at Bladnoch that sent us another good ten miles out of our way. Ten miles increased to twenty miles by the time I had got lost and taken the wrong turning in the dark on roads I didn't know. It was nearly eight o' clock before we arrived and after nine when I had finished unpacking. This place was noisy but in a good way. All you could hear for most of the night was the birds on the mud directly outside our cottage. The door and the front window of the cottage opened directly onto the sea front and people walked past frequently. Flash was always a good guard dog and made us jump one night as we were watching television. Someone walked past and he shot to the window barking like mad, he nearly knocked the TV over. For the rest of the week we decided to keep the curtains drawn.

On the Tuesday we went to watch a game at Greenock Morton. We went up the coast taking in Largs and Inverkip on the way. It was going to be an all-day affair so we took Flash with us. His meal that day consisted of chips and a battered sausage from a chip shop somewhere on the way and eaten in a car park at a local beauty spot. We parked the car in a spot where we could see it at the ground as the area was a bit rough to put it mildly. Flash was fine in the car and slept through the game after his long day out.

On the night before we were due to come home I took Flash for his final walk of the holiday. We'd packed everything up and I took him on my own as Brian was too tired to come with us. We went down a path that led to what passed as the coastline. It was a rough, unkempt area and was little more than scrubland. My aim was to keep to the path and this I did. Unfortunately Flash had other ideas. It was my fault really but I was distracted by a magnificent sight. Up on the brow of the hill and looking at me while I looked at it, was a large Red Deer stag, what a sight indeed. We looked at each other for what must have been no more than a minute. The stag ran off and I turned round to find Flash had disappeared. Whether he'd seen the stag himself and been spooked, I've no idea. I walked around the headland to find him up to his midriff in deep, thick mud. He looked at me with the kind of expression that said, "Look at me"! I had to take him home and explain to Brian what had happened. We had to unpack all the towels and then put Flash in the bath and scrub all the mud off him.

In July we went down to Suffolk to have one of our worst ever holidays. The cottage was in Hollesley. When we arrived the cottage hadn't been cleaned and none of the beds had been changed. The guy living next door was some sort of D.I.Y. freak and was sanding a wooden floor all hours of day and night. We played some music really loud to try and make him take a hint but to no avail. In the end we cut short our holiday and came home early from this place. We made a complaint to the cottage hire company when we arrived home and the following year the cottage had disappeared from their brochure.

Two months later and Flash went on his longest journey to date. Pendeen in Cornwall was our destination this time. The cottage once again left something to be desired, it being in the middle of a terrace. We couldn't get the TV to work and we ended up with no teletext for the week. Now this wouldn't have bothered most people but we liked teletext and its co-medium, ceefax, for the football scores and reports so we sulked all of Saturday night. The back garden of the cottage led to a path that went to the cliff top where some old tin mines were situated. Off we went with Flash. He must have taken a shine to a stone in someone's garden, the next minute we knew he had jumped down and picked up the said stone. He jumped back up to the path. On doing so he caught his testicles on a piece of barbed wire. Brilliant we thought, off to the vets we go. Anyway, no action was needed, upon inspection no serious injury had been sustained.

On the Sunday afternoon we took Flash for a walk down to the lighthouse. We had to retrace our steps at one point as Brian had lost his glasses, these were retrieved on a stone wall where he had been sat with Flash admiring the views.

The following year Flash only went on one holiday, the poor thing! Selsey in Sussex was to be 2005's destination. This really wasn't a cottage as such, it being a semi in a quiet residential area. The sea front was a ten minute walk away. It was ideal for walks and a little further on was Pagham Harbour. This was sensational for a walk but unfortunately with it being a nature reserve was more suited to humans than dogs. I walked around it late one night and met Brian who had Flash in tow. This was one place we thought we might visit again but we never did. We spent a magical late afternoon with Flash at Bramber Castle, nothing more than a pile of stones but it has a great park-like area where Flash was let off and free to roam. We took him down the side of the river at Arundel and watched the boats go back and forth. Another great river walk was at Midhurst, a delightful place full of interest and history. A picnic was had on the top of some burial mounds.

It would be another twelve months before we took Flash on another of his jaunts. A relatively long journey took us to a cottage in the village of Welcombe in Devon. This was the old bakery that had been split into two and was probably at this time the largest place we had ever stayed in. It was next door to the pub, which was handy for us but not so good for Flash. There was no garden and we couldn't find any suitable walks near the cottage for him. If we took him in the car though just down the road was Welcombe Mouth, a local beauty spot where some people were camping. The mouth in the title referred to the waterfall and there was a smaller downfall just a short distance away called Sandymouth. This was a great place for Flash and he went there nearly every day. One day he picked up his customary stone and I threw it over a small ridge for him to go and find it. We expected him back in a matter of seconds with it in his mouth as normal. A few minutes went by and we wondered what had happened to him, God forbid that he couldn't find it! We walked over the ridge to investigate. No sign of any dog. We didn't panic, we knew full well that Flash wouldn't have gone far when a stone was at stake. On going nearer to the waterfall we found Flash. He was up to his neck in water, in fact he was floating. He'd obviously fell in running for the stone and couldn't get back out again on his own. The pool he was in was only about three feet in circumference but was deep, probably about five feet. I scrambled down and hauled him out by the scruff of his neck. He promptly thanked me by shaking and drenching me in water. The stone was never seen again I might add.

This holiday was another Saturday to Saturday affair and we stopped at a football game at Appledore on the way down. This was an ideal set-up for Flash and we walked him around the pitch a couple of times at half time. Morwenstow was a nice place with a cliff-top church and some great fields to walk around. We had a great time finding the cliff face hideout that some local vicar had made for himself during the Victorian age.

September of the same year saw us undertake another long trip. A small cottage in Marazion overlooking St Michael's Mount. This was really small but the location was spectacular. The adjoining field had an eclectic mix of horses and donkeys in it. They were friendly enough with humans but we never let Flash go anywhere near them. Flash, by his standards, had a fairly quiet holiday this time out. The highlight for us was seeing a badger in full view in the garden. For a couple of nights we put some of Flash's dog food out and observed through the windows. Nothing was seen but both mornings afterwards the food had gone, probably a local fox we thought. We got talking with a local in the village and she told us to throw some peanuts down in the garden. This was by now our last night there so it was all or nothing. A full bag of peanuts was scattered all around the garden on the grass late at night. Sure enough at about ten o' clock we had our visitor who stayed until he'd eaten the lot. I say he but it could quite easily have been a she, it was far too dark to notice.

After having two long journeys down to the south-west, the following year we decided to go up to Scotland twice. We'd been to Isle of Whithorn previously and had really liked the area. It was quiet and the roads were also quiet and it was easy to get to, turn left at Dumfries being the very general directions. Rather than the Isle of Whithorn, this time we stopped in Whithorn itself. The cottage was superb, quite big with even a piano installed. We tried the usual corny thing with it, making a noise and seeing if Flash would bark or even howl at us. He just stood and looked at us like we were deranged or something, we probably were! The cottage had an enormous garden and Flash was largely left to his own devices while he was in it. It was fully enclosed although the wall was a little too small for our liking and we suspected that if Flash had took it onto himself he could have quite easily cleared it. Again we stopped at a game on-route, this time bang on the coast at a place called Creetown. We'd picked a good one again for Flash and it was far more entertaining taking him a walk around the pitch than watching the game itself. On the Wednesday we took Flash down to St Ninian's Cave in the pouring rain. We had the beach to ourselves, unsurprisingly, and we watched gannets diving into the sea. The following day was spent at Monreith at the Gavin Maxwell memorial and the ruins of Kirkmaiden Kirk. A great beach for Flash to do some digging on.

After going to Whithorn in July, three months later we were off up to bonny Scotland again. This time we went further north, the furthest we ever went in fact, to Blairgowrie. This place is famous for its raspberries and in the season is wall to wall with eastern Europeans picking them. We'd timed this holiday to "do" Pittodrie, the home of Aberdeen FC, who were at home on the Sunday. The day before we stopped at Stirling Albion on the way up but this time Flash had the ignominy of staying in the car for the duration of the game. Afterwards we took him into a local park and had the most expensive fish and chips we'd ever had, all of £5.00 each, daylight robbery. This cottage was almost perfect. So big we literally nearly got lost in it and kept going into the bedrooms instead of the kitchen or living room. We just let Flash have the run of the place. The housekeeper couldn't do enough for us, when we finally got into contact with her! We had a problem with the oven, you needed a degree in engineering in order to make it work. The housekeeper was constantly on the Internet despite her being elderly. This was in the days before you could use the Internet without disrupting your phone line and we had to wait hours before we could get through to her. It turned out we weren't that stupid after all and the previous occupants had reset the controls of the oven and messed it up so it wouldn't work at all. An electrician had to be called to reset it all. This cottage had another huge garden but Flash being the spoiled rotten dog he was still had to go his many walks. We first took him down to the river, but this had recently flooded and everywhere was very muddy underfoot. It would be our second visit to this cottage before we found the excellent walks that were literally across the road from the property. I took a photograph here that still adorns our living room wall. Flash had found a stone, no surprise there, and had dropped it into a small ornamental flower bed. He was stood next to it and his expression is one of, "Come on, throw it then".

The following April saw us in Scotland once again, in a place called Kippford. A cottage in a superb location but with an unenclosed garden. We managed to enclose it ourselves by rearranging some fences. This garden was a paradise for wildlife with a resident male pheasant and a red squirrel. We watched the squirrel run around the tree branches and took Flash on walks around the bay and through some woods near Dalbeattie, the nearest town of any size. Here we found a local butcher we were to go back to time and again for haggis amongst other things. I had some great walks on this holiday but I left Flash at home for most of them. I saw my first adder at Balcary Point. We took Flash to this place and he did some digging on the beach. Great memories.

Come August we were in Porlock for our second visit. This cottage had a huge garden. It was on an unmade lane and hidden behind some large gates. Flash had a great time exploring the garden. He was left to his devices most of the time but this holiday was spoilt by the weather. It rained a lot of the time. We caught a bus one day to the top of the famous Porlock Hill and walked back downhill through some woods that led directly to Tanglewood, the name of the cottage we were in. One night we walked down to the local pub, we were rewarded on our return journey by the sight of a tawny owl on a telegraph pole making its customary twit-too noises.

A couple of weeks later we were off again, this time back up to Blairgowrie, in the same cottage we had stayed in previously. The owners had responded to our problems on our previous visit with the oven, by installing a new state-of-art model. Nothing else in the cottage could be faulted. This time I took Flash across the road to explore the Fungarth Woods opposite. These were brilliant and we walked all the way around to the White Loch. I took him there when it was nearly dusk one night and he was spooked by a deer that shot out in front of us. If he had been off the lead I think he would have run home across the very busy A road. The last night we had there I walked all round the River Ericht past all the raspberry plantations. The river was lined on all sides by Himalayan Balsam and the smell was at times overpowering. We stopped off in Edinburgh on the Saturday of our return. Flash went round the lower slopes of Arthur's Seat and we then went to watch Edinburgh City at the Meadowbank Stadium.

A couple of weeks before Christmas we went all the way to Swansea to watch the Blades. It rained all the way down on the Friday night and when we got there a lot of villages were flooded, including the one we were stopping in. There were no walks at all where we were situated. On the Sunday I drove everyone to the Mumbles peninsula to the Worm's Head, a stunningly attractive place. Unfortunately it was snided with people and not really a good place for Flash. Neither was the cottage. It was an upside-down type of place and the living room was up a open spiral staircase, we had to keep an eye on Flash in case he fell through it. Luckily, this was only a three night stay. The cottage owner turned out to be some official at Swansea City and we were treated to free corporate hospitality at the stadium.

The year 2009 was another four vacation year for Flash. Once more up to Scotland we went in March for another three night stay. This cottage was right next to a busy road just outside the town of Kinross. We could hear the traffic most of the time. The adjoining farm was home to loads of finches and by walking through its farmyard we took Flash on a lovely walk. This was another football weekend and Cowdenbeath was visited on the Saturday and I went to Partick Thistle on the Sunday. This cottage was notable for being freezing and from this holiday onwards we started to take some portable heaters with us in the colder months.

One month later we went back to our previous cottage in Kippford. We had problems with the electricity this time and we had to get the caretaker out twice late at night to come and fix the problem. We had to keep an extra eye out for Flash this time as the fences we had used to enclose the garden the last time we were there had been removed, so the garden was fairly open at the front of the property. We caught the bus one night to Rockcliffe and walked back with Flash to Kippford. I had a particularly great wildlife day on the Monday. After walking around Balcary Bay and seeing an adder again in just about the same place as I had seen one on my previous visit, I then observed at close quarters a stoat. We stared at each other for some seconds and then it was off through the stone wall and into its hideout. In the evening we went for a drive towards New Abbey and saw a couple of deer in a field at the side of the road. Flash did his usual digging routine on the beach at Balcary Bay, one of our favourite places to take him on holiday anywhere.

In July we took a cottage in Palnackie, not far from Kippford, at very short notice and cheap. The rental was cheap for a reason and the cottage left a lot to be desired. Palnackie is home, apparently, to the World Flounder Tramping Championships and a nice walk to a viewpoint set up to mark the Millennium was Flash's easy walk from the cottage. We stopped for football on the way up at Annan and a great walk was found down to the river here, it being under the shade of the trees. We also parked the car here to keep Flash cool while he was in the car waiting for us. It wasn't very quiet for Flash because loads of teenage lads were jumping from a bridge into the river.

We made the mistake of buying him a new ball for the occasion but we forgot his age, he was by now fourteen, and we think this contributed to him becoming ill this holiday. The real reason though was undoubtedly walking him too far one afternoon in the unexpected heat after it had rained all the morning. He was quite ill for the rest of the holiday and we thought that we had brought on the end of his life at one point.

Nevertheless, come September we took him down to Morecombelake in Dorset and he was none the worse for his ordeal. This was a very strange cottage. The setting was good, albeit slightly up a steep hill and the cottage itself being up some steep steps from the car parking area. Across the road was a great walk for me but we were wiser now about Flash and he never went too far this holiday. En-route we stopped at Axminster for football. Flash was walked at the side of the pitch a couple of times here but again it was hot for him. We started to walk him over St Aldham's Head, near Worth Maltravers but it was too hot for him one afternoon and we curtailed our walk for a visit to the Square and Compass for some beer and some much needed water for Flash. This cottage was furnished weirdly. It had the finest collection of 70's Tupperware we'd ever seen, together with an old dentist's chair in one of the bedrooms.

By 2010, Flash wasn't as mobile as he used to be. A combination of arthritis and old age were starting to take its toll. Consequently the cottage and the locations were picked with him in mind. The first holiday of 2010 was at a farm near a village called Little Witley in Worcestershire. The cottage was big but had some sort of problem with the electrics because you could hear a scratching noise at night from behind the walls. The farm itself was an asparagus farm and had machines that omitted loud bangs to scare away the pigeons, luckily these didn't operate during the night! This holiday was a wet one and Flash's walk was a muddy one up a track on the farm.

The second holiday closely followed the first at the end of April. By now we had started going Friday to Friday so we didn't have to stop on the way for a football game. I normally went on my own to a game on the following day. This time my destination was Eyemouth. The ground was on the clifftop overlooking the town. A great place to take Flash and walk him around the cliff. We found a walk in some woods opposite a supposedly haunted castle. No spirits were seen, only squirrels. We took him down at the side of the River Tweed near Innerleithen. The cottage itself was near a place called Clovenfords, near Peebles.

In June we made a bad mistake in our choice of destination. This was another last-minute decision. Springholm is a village on the busy A75 between Dumfries and Stranraer. The "cottage", and I use the metaphor loosely, was attached to the owners property, something we never stopped in before or since. The garden was nice enough but the owner was in it all the time we spent there. The cottage's description in the brochure said it was within walking distance of the village and the pub. The trouble was there was no footpath and the road was the A75, extremely busy with huge lorries all of the day and night. We didn't stop long. We realised that we had exhausted all the sites in the area and we were stuck for something to do. We came home very early on the Wednesday. We couldn't even find a decent walk for Flash. The best place we went to was Morton Castle where we had the place to ourselves and the view and setting were pretty spectacular.

The last holiday of the year was much better. The cottage was nice although spoilt slightly by us having to park on the road. It was situated at the bottom of the huge hill in Sidford in East Devon. Again it was Friday to Friday and I even managed a game on the Friday night at Crediton. Flash liked this cottage and he was left alone in it a lot more than previous holidays. He particularly liked the settee because it was low down for him to jump on, the same as the one we had at home. It absolutely threw it down on a couple of the days we were there. Perversely, on one of the other days, I got sunburnt. We had some problems with the car on this holiday and had to go into Exeter to fetch another one to get about with and to get us home. Ours was repaired and delivered back up north the week later.

Another four trips were made in 2011. By now Flash was a very old boy indeed. The first one was to Bradford. No, not to the dump in Yorkshire but to Bradford-on-Avon in Wiltshire. This was to coincide with my 50th birthday. Walks for Flash consisted of going up and down the side of the canal. I tried in vain to do every pub in the town on the Thursday, the fateful day, but some of them were closed so didn't manage it.

One month later we decided to go much nearer home and went to a village called Roxby situated near Staithes in North Yorkshire. I went on a few long walks on the coast path but by now Flash was fairly content exploring the large garden the property had. He had some sport by chasing the chickens that found their way through the hedge.

At the end of August we went to Somerton in Somerset. The cottage was the nearest place we could find at short notice to enable myself to watch the Blades at Yeovil on the following day, Saturday. This was the biggest mistake we ever made as regard holiday venues. While the property was not actually attached to the owner's property, it was bang next door and shared a garden at the front. There was nowhere whatsoever for Flash to go his walk, however short it had now become. To cap it all Flash got stung on the leg by a wasp. A younger dog would probably have just shrugged it off and indeed that was the advice the local vet gave us on the phone. However, because of his age it really made Flash ill and we thought at one point we wouldn't be bringing him home alive. The cottage had a stone floor and Flash at times struggled to keep his feet on it. The properties television wasn't fit for purpose and even when the owner went and bought another one especially for us it didn't make our mood much better. We didn't stay nowhere near as long as we had booked for and came home on the Tuesday.

The last holiday of 2011 was at Grange-over-Sands in Lancashire. This was a very unusual upside down house with the bedrooms downstairs and the living room upstairs. This actually suited us and Flash very well and there was the added bonus of walks on the promenade for Flash that were flat and easy to get to in the car. The weather did its best to spoil things though and after raining all the way there it hardly stopped for a couple of days. On the Thursday we decided to take Flash to Silecroft, a small place on the Cumbrian coast. We planned on taking some photos of him on the beach, thinking that it may be the last time he ever saw the sand. Flash had a whale of a time but I forgot to take the camera with me and left it in the bag on the chair when we went out.

Christmas came and went and it was now 2012. Flash was still in reasonable health despite now being some seventeen years old. In March we went to Flamborough Head just for the weekend. Flash's walks were of the very short variety by now. The cottage was bang next door to a café and was ideally situated for taking Flash just around the headland. The weather was glorious and I actually got sunburnt walking to Bempton and back.

A month later we went a bit further up the coast to Sleights, just outside Whitby. The cottage was in a great location but we couldn't find any short walks for Flash. Nevertheless, he enjoyed himself around the large garden. The garden was just grass and had not been touched in a few years, a bit like some parts of the cottage, whose cleanliness left a lot to be desired. One day we took him to the beach at Sandsend. To our surprise and delight he started to dig like he did when he was younger. We took some photos with tears in our eyes because we knew it could be the last time he ever did this. So it turned out. This was to be Flash's last holiday. We were due to go to near Dunbar in Scotland in September. Flash never made it.

Flash used to love his holidays. He would get excited when he saw us getting the cases down from the loft and he knew he was going somewhere different. The journey itself sometimes took it out of him. Even on the following day he was sometimes a bit quieter than normal but by the second day he would be raring to go.

During all these holidays I took loads of photographs of Flash. They read like a catalogue of his life. Brian and I look back on them now with fondness and sometimes some tears.

Day Trips

Due to the fact that we never had a car for the early part of Flash's life he never really went for many day trips. Later on we hired cars for holidays to start with and then progressed slightly to getting one for a weekend occasionally. Quite a few trips we had involved taking in a football game on the same day. In July 2002 we got a car to enable us to go to Eastbourne on holiday, Flash wasn't going with us but instead was making his first visit tothe kennels, something he really hated. We must have felt a little guilty because on the preceding Sunday we took him with us to Elton Vale in Bury, Lancashire. For some reason, now unknown, this game was played on a Sunday. It wasn't too bad a place for Flash with some walks going through some woodland next to it. After Flash went into Kennels a couple of times when Brian and I went on holidays we decided he wasn't suitable for such delights. He looked at us so accusingly we felt too guilty to leave him.

With the day out being a success we said we would repeat the process again at some other games. Nevertheless, it would be May Day Bank Holiday before we did this again. We got the car from Saturday to Wednesday, taking in the bank holiday Monday. Hall Road Rangers, based in Dunswell, near Hull was the destination on the Saturday. We combined it with a visit to The Deep in Hull, which was a big disappointment. Flash stayed in the car while we were there but we took him out at half time at the football. We stopped at the country park underneath the Humber Bridge on the way back to reward him for his patience.

August 2004 brought with it a new football season. A trip out to Formby seemed to be a good idea early on. We planned this as a good day out for all three of us this time. We walked Flash around the sand dunes and visited the red squirrel colony where we had some great shots of the little blighters.

The same season but later on in April we had the use of a car for a few days courtesy of a good friend. Flash attended his first midweek game. He stayed in the car for most of the time but went a walk at half-time. We had a slight scare on the way. The car was fairly old and some of the front seat fittings were exposed. We were driving through Halifax on the way to the game at Ovenden West Riding, (based in Illingworth high up in the hills), when Flash started wailing. He'd trapped his paw in the front passenger seat rider. We had to stop to free him but he was non-the-worse for his little ordeal.

From a sporting point, this was Flash's last trip until August 2008. In February 2008 we got a brand new Skoda Roomster. This was like its name implied, a car with loads of room inside it. This was why we chose the model. The following August we took Flash to Horncastle in Lincolnshire. This was a successful day out and Flash saw most of the game as he stayed most of the time around the pitch whilst the game was taking place. Football wise, we were a bit limited as to where Flash could be taken, he couldn't have been taken into a proper stadium for instance.

As it was, the same season but in March we took him on the fairly longer journey up to Thornaby on Teeside. This was a fabulous place for Flash. The ground and the surrounding area had long since gone wild and was overgrown with weeds and walks through woods and the like. To cap a great day out we won the bottle of wine in the raffle.

The following October the much shorter trip up to Todmordon was undertaken. This ground was situated at the side of the canal and was again highly suitable for Flash to have a wander up the canal path. October must have been the month for such trips because the next year Flash was taken to two games in one day. The first was at Leeds United's training ground at Thorpe Arch near Wetherby. Flash had to go a walk before we went here because we didn't think they would like us taking the dog a walk around the pitch at such a place. In the afternoon Flash went to the far more suitable surroundings of Kirkheaton Rovers, which was little more than a pitch with plenty of waste ground around it for his little bit of exercise. Flash was fed on fish and chips that afternoon.

Once again in October, of 2011, Flash went on his travels again. Market Rasen was the destination this time. We stopped off in some woods nearby and went there again after the game. We walked him up the side of the pitch a couple of times, totally ignoring the sign saying no dogs allowed on the ground. No one stopped us and to be honest Flash wasn't the only dog in attendance. After the game in said woods we had a great close-up view of a green woodpecker.

As well as football we also watch rugby league. Flash, however, only ever went to one of these games. This was in May 2008 when we took him to Scarborough for the day. It was a fairly hot day so he spent the time around the pitch in the shade rather than in the car.

Escapades & Lucky Escapes

While he was still fairly young Flash brought the house down, or rather the curtain rail on the patio door. He used to jump up sometimes when he went a walk and this day he caught the curtain and brought the lot down. He did this because his lead was hung up on the side of the door. To cap it all he did exactly the same the following day. His lead was promptly moved to another location.

Also, about this time Flash had his tail caught in the kitchen door. He had a quite distinctive curly tail and had the habit of following Brian in and out of the kitchen. On this day Brian closed the door too quickly and Flash had not fully gone through it. He yelped, obviously, and ran into the living room at full speed. After a full inspection of his tail, no harm was found to have been done. We did, however, think in later years that this episode had made his tail even curlier!

In September 1999 Flash had his only operation, for a small growth on his ear. It was nothing major but at the time we were not very well off finance wise so we took him to the PDSA to have it done. When we went to fetch him he was still a bit groggy and he was so cute with a pink bandage around his head. Everyone in the waiting room expressed their concerns for him and agreed with us about his cuteness. He just wanted to exit the place as soon as possible. For a couple of days he had to have a plastic collar on to stop him scratching it. This was the first time we let him onto the settee to sleep. He would continue to sleep on the settee for the rest of his life.

We had a couple of minor episodes with vehicles on our road, which is a cul-de-sac. Luckily the cars were travelling fairly slow and were able to stop before any real damage was done. However, whilst I was in Dundee one weekend in November 2002, Brian took Flash out on his own. He took him round the lump so to speak, a short walk up a path between the old people's home and some trees. He made the mistake of letting Flash off thinking he could get him back. He also made the further mistake of going too near to the main road and Flash saw someone who Brian described as looking like me. Flash must have also thought this and shot across the main road. Brian described the scene to me later that night when I phoned to see if everything was OK, the scream of brakes and Brian's heart being in his mouth. Luckily the driver managed to stop in time and Flash was quickly put back on his lead, never to be let off again either in this location or when Brian took him out on his own.

We had a certain type of smoke alarm in the house, the type that screws into a light socket and gets charged by the electricity therein. It was prone to go off for no apparent reason sometimes and also it went off if you accidentally flicked the light switch more than once. Flash hated it but we persevered with it for a number of years. We came back one Saturday night from the pub to find Flash had disappeared. We couldn't find him anywhere. Eventually, we did find him of course, he was forced to be somewhere in the house after all! He was stuck at the back of the washer, tangled in the wires. He must have forced himself into this position by being terrified of something. We figured it must have been the bloody smoke alarm. We still didn't replace it though after all that. A couple of years later Flash had a couple of episodes where he had something resembling a fit and he keeled over. He recovered just about straight away. Our explanation for this again was the bloody smoke alarm. This time it was the last straw and the offending article was deposited in the bin.

On a few occasions we left Flash at home while we went on holiday abroad, (or on a couple of occasions, Eastbourne), being looked after by a friend of ours, Phil. This guy used to come over to our house mainly on Sundays for his Sunday dinner. He also stayed a few times with us at Christmas. He lived on his own and had always done. This had made him somewhat eccentric, to put it politely. He had a certain nervous cough and would also sneeze a lot at the drop of a hat. Flash had a thing about both these instances later in his life and we blamed Phil for this. If anybody coughed or sneezed, he would run off and hide behind the settee.

At one time our next door neighbours also had a dog, called Tigger, after the character in the children's Winnie the Pooh books. Tigger was a Jack Russell. Tigger and Flash never liked each other and on the odd occasion they met face-to-face fought ferociously. They had to be pulled apart more than once.

The incidents that occurred on holiday at Palnackie, Isle of Whithorn, Welcombe and Somerton have been described in detail in other chapters in this book but these four episodes were relatively minor compared to Flash's main brush with death one Friday afternoon in November 2007. I took him on the bus to Midhope crossroads to walk back from there at the side of Underbank Dam. This path runs alongside the main A616 road. We'd done this walk a few times and it was fairly pleasant. There was one particular section where Flash had to go on the lead because the path was directly alongside the road and with a small wall that Flash could easily jump over if so inclined. Anyway on this day I was too slow or Flash ran off too quick, whichever. Before I knew it he was at the wall, I shouted but to no avail. The incident lived up to his name, it happened in a flash. The next thing I knew he was in the middle of the road with a line of lorries and cars heading for him. Whether the lorry driver ever saw him I don't know to this day. I watched in total horror as the first lorry went over Flash.

I tried to scream but no sound came out of my mouth. Flash was there in the road ready to be squashed. He somehow made it to the pavement before the second lorry bore down on him and I got to him expecting to see the worst. I thought if I can just lay him at the side of the road and see what damage had been done. Miraculously, he looked OK. He jumped up onto the wall and I examined him. He had no marks on him and he looked OK, he looked OK, yes he looked OK. I kept repeating it to myself, he'd just jumped on the wall, remember. No one had stopped at the side of the road, (whether anyone had actually seen anything I don't know), and no bus was due to return home. I only had one alternative, to walk Flash back home the way I had intended all along. I had my mobile with me and phoned Brian to tell him the dog had been run over. I never stopped to think, I could have caused him to have a heart attack! Flash was slow and very quiet all the way back but he seemed to be walking alright. I had shouted at him and this probably caused him to be quiet as he never liked that at all. I got him back home and we both examined him, nothing untoward. We phoned the vet and explained the situation and agreed to take him to Barnsley to be checked out. We didn't have a car in those days and no neighbour was around for them to take us. We caught the next bus, which was about an hour later.

The buses around Stocksbridge have never been very reliable and prone to not turning up from day to day. However, this one duly turned up and we were off. Flash was still quiet but still looked fine. At a place called Gilroyd, this side of Barnsley, the bus broke down and couldn't go any further. What a great day we were having! We waited nearly an hour for a replacement bus to come out, we were the only passengers on it so they didn't rush or anything. Eventually we got Flash to the vets. He checked him out and couldn't find anything wrong with him. Just one thing though, that will be £40.00 please, was his verdict, we paid it happily. When we got him home we could have strangled him!

It turned out that the lorry must have gone straight over the top of Flash and he'd had the sense to duck right at the last moment. We studied lorries long and hard and just about every one we saw never had enough room underneath for a squirrel to get under it never mind a dog. Someone or something, depending on your religion, must have been looking out for him that day. We could laugh about it and we still do to this day even though Flash has now gone but I never want to go through a day like it again in my life.

Getting Old

In the end Flash suffered with arthritis. He had it in all four legs but the front two were the worst. When he was younger he jumped over countless walls and we played a lot of ball with him. He used to run up and down at the cemetery until he could hardly run any more. Whether this made a difference to him in later life is open to speculation. The holiday in Palnackie was the first time we thought he was on his way out. We bought him a new ball, which was a big mistake. He'd not played ball for a while and it took it out of him. One day we also took him a fairly long walk in the sun. The following day he was very lethargic and he stayed like that for the rest of the holiday, (luckily only a couple of days), and for a couple of days when we returned home. Happily though, he made a recovery and the Palnackie "incident" was a good three years before he finally succumbed to old age.

Flash used to sleep on Brian's bed sometimes, until he finally couldn't get up onto it anymore. One night Brian was awakened by the sound of Flash screaming in pain. I awoke as well and rushed into the next bedroom. Flash was holding one of his front paws in an unnatural pose and it was obviously not in his correct position and causing him some discomfort. We didn't know what to do really. Should we call out the emergency vet or not? We decided not to eventually and Flash seemed to improve slightly and be in less pain. Both of us never went back to sleep though that night. Straight away as soon as the vets were open we called the number and we made an emergency appointment to see the vet at Deepcar. We took him down in the car and the vet gave him two injections and some tablets. The following day Flash was his normal self and didn't seem any different so whatever was in the injections certainly worked.

The weekend break down at Somerton in August 2011 was a terrible break in truth. In hindsight we should have never gone. The "cottage" was attached to the owner's property, something we never entertain normally. However, I was going to Yeovil for the football and it was the nearest place we could find. In the garden there was a fruit tree and it was surrounded by wasps. We naturally avoided going near it and just killed the sods that came into the house. One afternoon Flash came into the cottage holding up a paw. At first we thought it might be another bout of his old complaint. After examination though we concluded that he had been stung by a wasp. The owner himself had two dogs so we went next door and he kindly gave us the vet's emergency number. After talking to the vet he told us that there was not much he could do but just to make sure Flash didn't have any adverse reaction to the sting and keep an eye on him and the symptoms would wear off eventually. Sure enough he was OK.

The End

The end itself came rather suddenly. For about six months he'd stopped going upstairs and it had been about nine months before he'd jumped onto the bed. Nevertheless, he still went his small walk and he was eating more than he'd ever done, sometimes having a full three tins of food a day. On Saturday July 21st he came and brushed my leg like he used to do when he'd been a long walk for instance. The following weekend we took him for a "walk" on the Saturday and we knew, we just knew. He could hardly walk and it was his last outing. We let him linger until the Wednesday but maybe we should have taken him sooner. We took him in the car to the vets on the same day as my late mother's birthday. Tears are streaming down my face as I type this some seven months afterwards. Imagine what I was like on the day itself. It was certainly one of the worst days of my life and one of the worst things I've ever had to do.

Overall though, there is no doubt that Flash had a fantastic life, how many dogs go on thirty-two vacations? Some humans don't manage nowhere near as many. This number included long weekends mostly for football purposes. Brian and I can be proud of the life and care we gave him.

As a footnote, we eventually decided to get another dog some two months after Flash went. We were undecided at first with us both getting older. The house was just too quiet though and so we took the plunge. We couldn't get a puppy for love nor money. Only pedigrees were available at extortionate costs that we couldn't afford. My friend Anita eventually put us in touch with a girl called Theresa who gets dogs from Romania and passes them on to vetted households. We were told there was a puppy available in Romania but we were told it had a lot of health issues surrounding it. We saw some photos of him on the Internet. His name was Bracken and he was three months old. We had to wait a further month before he was due to make his long journey over to Great Britain and ultimately Sheffield. He then got held up for a further two weeks because there weren't enough dogs to put on the lorry to make the journey viable. His health issues included having distemper and parvo virus. Luckily, he was a survivor and made a full recovery from both diseases. Eventually he arrived and we went to see him. His first reaction to my voice was to cower under the table and poo and wet himself, not good! However, we fell in love with him at first sight and we knew we wanted him. We visited him a further two times and left some old clothes with him so he could get used to our smell. When we went for the third time he initially barked before running into his cage. He came to us on bonfire night, not a good night to have a new dog. Nevertheless, he slept all night and wouldn't come out of his basket. He came on this night for a reason. He had just caught kennel cough from some of the dogs at Theresa's and the following day we had to take him to the vets for this to be sorted out. We had to put his food very near to him because he wouldn't move far. We had a few qualms about him and wondered if we'd made the right decision. However, as I type he has come on no end. He now looks forward to his walks and we even let him off the lead occasionally. He will make a good dog and we look forward to giving him as good a life as we did with Flash.

Belle, A Dog's Tail
By
Karen Taylor

Karen Taylor lives on a small, windswept island off the west coast of Scotland and most days wishes she didn't. She lives alone now that her son has rather selfishly gone off to university…if you don't count the two dogs and five cats. Happy to perpetuate the stereotype of a forty year old single woman obsessed with animals, she embraces her spinsterhood with passion. She is a published writer, both digital and mainstream, and is proud to have written something her son can finally read.

Karen has chosen to write about her Staffordshire Bull Terrier, Belle, in the hope that a positive picture of life with a Staffie might change some opinions on the so called 'devil dogs'.

The thing is, Belle was never meant to be.

What she *was* meant to be was a chocolate Labrador puppy. Cute, wriggly and absolutely, definitely not a Staffordshire Bull Terrier – and an ugly one at that.

It was my only child's tenth birthday and, having recently split up with his father, I was eager to get him whatever his little heart desired and thus alleviate my crushing guilt in breaking up his family unit. Fortunately the split with his father was possibly the most amicable in history and he was fully on board with this plan – especially as, in retrospect, was that all he had to do was contribute to costs and not actually do any of the hard work.

All the glory, none of the hassle!

It was on a Saturday a week or so before his birthday that my son, my mother, my sister and myself sallied forth to go and view a litter of chocolate Labradors my sister had heard about at a local farm (as it was to come out years later an *actual* puppy farm) and we were soon knee deep in nine of the charming little devils. They were gorgeous. Glossy, fat, chocolately brown….and not one of them attracted my son's attention. They climbed all over him, tumbled all over each other, played, kissed, tugged at his clothes and did everything but jump up and down holding little signs saying 'Pick me! Pick me!' and he did nothing but kneel in the straw with them and enjoy a tussle and romp.

I, on the other hand, was made of sterner stuff and I had things to do. I lovingly informed him he had five minutes to make up his mind or we were going without a puppy and he looked up at me and informed me just as firmly that 'None of them feel like mine, mum.' and made it abundantly clear by a determined squint of his eye that he would be losing no sleep over the puppies that night but I damn well would be.

And every subsequent night until the puppy that felt like his was found.

I want to make it clear that I am not one of these parents that bow to their child's every whim. I have, and still do, put my foot down with firm regularity and have no problem saying no to requests if I don't agree with them. I'm not his friend, I'm his parent. However, I am also a parent that listens to their kid and treats his opinion with respect, something I firmly believe has led us to nineteen years together without a single proper row, and I recognised that he'd made up his mind.

The puppies in front of him were cute but none of them were inspiring him to make a lifetime commitment of love, care and companionship. Torn between pride at his maturity and frustration that he couldn't just for once be a normal, shallow child and grab the first pretty with both hands I gritted my teeth, forced a smile at the man showing us the litter and apologised for taking up his time.

To his credit – or more likely anxious to avoid his generous remuneration trotting out the door – the gentleman smiled benevolently and asked if we would like to see a litter of King Charles Spaniel pups that were conveniently located just two stables over. The child's eyes lit up, my heart sank (I've never been a fan of the breed) and we sidled over to have a look. Half an hour later and we had achieved the same result – the puppies were delighted with the visit, the child was amused but not smitten and everyone else just wanted to go home. We made our excuses and left and, to my irritation, my sister suggested we pop into the pet shop on the way home to see if there was anything on the notice board there.

The child was getting a little teary eyed at this point – unusual enough that my crushing guilt raised its ugly head again – so when a small postcard announced the existence of a thirteen and a half week old Staffie for sale in the next town over I gave in with barely a whimper. We called and were told she was still available for viewing and were welcome to pop over that afternoon. After a short, tense drive we pulled up in front of a small terrace house on a well-kept estate and meandered up the garden path to the sound of a veritable cacophony of barks and yips from inside. Entering the house was an excercsise in good manners and restraint – I have never smelt anything like it in my life.

We entered straight into the kitchen where crammed into the corner was a mini tower block of six dog cages each with a puppy – or puppies – inside. Three adult dogs ran around, accompanied by two puppy pit bulls, and the smell of them, their bodily functions, the dinner the woman had bubbling on the stove and the odour from the unemptied cat litter tray at the foot of the tower of cages was nearly overpowering.

However none of this registered with the child. He took one look at the white and ginger quivering bundle in one of the top cages and it was all over. He'd found his dog. Sure she was boss eyed, knock kneed and seemed to have no control over her tongue, but that didn't seem to matter. To him she was the most beautiful dog he'd ever seen and he couldn't wait to get his eager little hands on her.

I was less enthused. I questioned the woman who had shown us in intently – how was her temperament? Which out of the dogs milling around were her parents? Was she *meant* to look like that?

Belle's story was depressing and typical for her breed I later found out. Aside from having the misfortune of being born into the care of, literally, a back street breeder she had also been born at the height of the craze for Staffordshire Bull Terriers and had been bred for security and protection. At the tender age of just over three months she had already been returned to her breeder three times as being wholly unsuitable for the purpose.

I looked at the tiny handful my son was seated on the floor with, clutched to his chest, and the way she was desperately trying to wriggle out of sight inside his t-shirt. My anxiety at what I thought I knew about her breed abated somewhat – it was hard to picture the small creature currently tail up as she disappeared inside the neck of his shirt being a danger to anyone, let alone actually doing them harm.

I looked back at the breeder and tried to remain on track – how well socialised was she? Were there any health issues we should be aware of? Were there verifiable medical records we could see? Could we see the Kennel Club documentation that the woman kept boasting of every other breath?

All my sensible questions became moot when my child piped up from the floor – his puppy's name was Belle and when could he take her home?

I looked at the kid, I looked at the dog and then I looked at the woman now beaming at me with expectant smugness. I sighed and reluctantly enquired when the Ugly Puppy would be able to leave. Despite her already been out to three homes and then returned we were told that she needed one final check at the vets and she would be ready in the middle of the following week. The date given fell by pure chance on the actual date of my son's birthday and, choosing to view this as a positive omen, I forked over the holding fee and agreed we would be over after school the following Wednesday to take possession.

I'm fortunate that my son has always been very mature in many ways and, aside from natural excitement at the new addition, the next week passed fairly peaceably as we prepared the house. We already had two older Rhodesian Ridgebacks, Tuko and Clyde, and I was fairly sanguine about their reaction to Belle – at worst she would be tossed about a bit, at best they'd take to her on sight and adopt her immediately as their own. Either way it could be worked around and we could accommodate whatever changes would need to be made.

After school on my son's birthday we piled into his father's car and went to collect the Ugly Puppy. The smell was just as remarkable as it had been on our first visit but infinitely more bearable now that I knew this would be the last time we would be subjected to it. In a remarkably swift transaction, Belle was foisted onto my son, I was relieved of the balance of her fee and we were all but shoved back out the door now the proud guardians of what would turn out to be the world's most depressed puppy.

In many respects, right from the word go, it became apparent that Belle was not going to conform to the stereotype for her breed. She was the epitome of love and gentleness with my son and came alive in his presence – unfortunately, for a long time, with everyone else she was the most miserable, depressed baggage ever to grace a home.

She lay pressed against my son's leg the entire car ride home, utterly silent, and endured her introduction to my thoroughly bemused older dogs with resigned stoicism and then promptly draped herself over my son's lap for the rest of the night, eyeing him and his birthday pizza with equal devotion. I tried to convince myself that she was just withdrawn with the shock of another home and that her ambivalence to everything but my child was a manifestation of this. This turned out to be a wildly optimistic, and forlorn, hope. Belle had evidently decided that there was exactly one person in her new reality that deserved her attention and devotion and that was my son, everyone else was irrelevant.

The first night she came home I had agreed a compromise with the child when it came to bedtime and he didn't want to be separated from the new love of his life. She would be allowed to sleep in his room, but she must sleep in her own bed. Under no circumstances would she be allowed to sleep with him. This was non-negotiable. I would brook no arguments.

I'm pretty sure you've guessed where this is going.

Bedtime arrived and the child was tucked lovingly into his bed…and a small ginger and white missile shot under his duvet, down to his feet and wrapped around his shins and clung on like a limpet when I tried to drag her out. I swiftly re-evaluated the situation, decided I was far too lazy to insist on the previous non-negotiable terms of puppy training and left them to it.

This arrangement continued until the day he left home some eight years later.

The next morning was also a good indication of how life was to be from now on. I separated the pair of them with difficulty when his lift arrived for school and the moment he disappeared out the front door Belle entered what can only be described as a melancholy decline. She slunk miserably into the living room, ignored the other dogs and curled up grunting mournfully to herself for the next six hours. Nothing could persuade her life was worth living. I tried cuddles, food, firm direction to the garden to come and play – she was inconsolable.

The first day was spent going between the Ugly Puppy (bonding between us was to take considerable time due to her absolute refusal to look at me as anything but the dreadful monster that habitually separated her from her love and, occasionally, a necessary evil that supplied food) and the internet, frantically researching Staffies and their recognised quirks and traits.

By the time it was necessary to go and collect my son from school I was convinced we had been sold a dud and there was a lot more to her frequent returns to her breeder than her inability to make a security dog.

Having promised the child that I would bring his puppy to meet him from school I scooped her up, because of *course* she refused to walk, and took her on to the bus for the half hour trip to meet him. She spent the entire journey seated beside me, resolutely refusing to look at me and point blank ignoring everyone who tried to make a fuss of her. By the end of the journey I was seriously considering trying to swap her for a hamster.

We arrived at the school gates in good time and she planted herself at my feet, scowling at the floor and hunched like a little gargoyle as she chuntered away to herself at this new hell she was being forced to endure. The bell sounded for the end of school and she didn't so much as twitch when four hundred plus pre-teens started to stream out of the gates and thunder past her. In fact she didn't look up until she heard a shout of "Belle! Look, there's my dog! It's Belle!" as my son led eight or so of his very closest friends in a rush towards her and then it was like an electric wire had been directly applied to her hindquarters. Her whole body went rigid and then she was up on all four paws, eyes bulging in rapture and tongue flopping uncontrollably as her boy charged. She strained at her leash, danced frenetically as he ran and then flung herself into his outstretched arms with whimpers of sheer joy.

By comparison my own "Hi, love, had a good day?" was somewhat underwhelming, but happily as they were both ignoring me I got away with it.

Belle was a different dog. She greeted my son with rapturous joy normally only displayed when warriors return from a hard fought war, enthusiastically introduced herself to his friends and generally behaved like a puppy should. She even trotted beautifully at his heels on her lead when we took our eventual leave and made our way home.

I eyed her narrowly and thought mean and unbecoming thoughts for a mature woman of certain years.

That night she was playful, loving and a general delight to be around. She and my son fell ever deeper into what would become a lifelong love and I knew that we'd made a good decision in bringing her into our home. I put aside thoughts of sourcing a hamster replacement and decided that she'd just needed some time and understanding to adjust...until the next morning when the whole sorry cycle was repeated all over again.

The door had barely had time to close behind the child before she morphed into Greta Garbo and took to her bed in another fit of despair. I tried *everything*. The older dogs tried to coax her to play, to come out to the garden, just to lift her head so we all knew that at least she was still breathing, nothing worked. At school collection time I once again carried her out of the door, onto the bus and to the school gates. The only changes from the day before was that now she had added pitiful cringing and flinching to her repertoire and could apparently shiver miserably at will, even in pools of warm autumnal sunshine.

Ignoring the suspicious stares from the other parents as they looked between me and the sorrowful creature at my feet, I waited expectantly for the sound of my son's dulcet tones and, sure enough, the moment Belle registered his voice her transformation was nothing short of miraculous. She went from being the poster child for the RSPCA to being 'Puppy Most Likely…' at Crufts and fairly crackled with energy and delight as they were reunited. I handed over the leash, took his ridiculously heavy school bag and reminded myself grimly as I followed in their wake that I loved my child and there was nothing I would not do to secure his happiness.

Even if it turned out that I would putting up with the world's most passive aggressive dog for the next fifteen years.

They spent a wonderful next few days together thanks to the half term holidays and by the time the next Monday arrived when he was due back at school it was like Belle had always lived with us. She had come to terms with the fact that there were other people around her that she had to at least tolerate, but all the love she had stored in her tiny body was for my son and him alone. His friends she seemed to view as extensions of him and was ecstatic when they came to the house to play. It didn't matter what they did – Playstation, football, TV, wrestling, eating – as long as she was included she was happy. My son was over the moon with his dog – she was everything he could hope for and more. I've never believed in soul mates or destiny but in this particular case I can be persuaded. Without really doing anything special to bond, these two had found each other and they created their own little universe where anyone else could only hope for brief glimpses but could never stay.

I, on the other hand, was less enthused. In many respects Belle was the perfect puppy. She never chewed or was destructive, accidents around the house were rare, and she was never aggressive and was ridiculously quiet and calm. She was, however, not inclined to form relationships with anyone else outside my son.

There was also the problem of exercise. Belle did not do it. She did not like to walk, she did not like to explore, and she point blank refused to play fetch or tug or anything else that did not directly involve my son. This was problematic for many reasons but mainly because he was still too young to walk her by himself and when he came home from school it was dark, he was hungry and there were a plethora of things that needed doing other than walking a dog that should have been going in the morning with the other canine occupants of the house.

In this, as in so many things, Belle got her own way.

A compromise was reached where the older dogs were walked as usual in the morning, Belle stayed at home triumphant – or planning ways to bring about her own untimely demise dependant on how suspiciously I was viewing her that particular day – and then when it became time to pick up the child, I took her onto the bus and carried her to meet him and then handed over the lead and we walked her to the local park where she lovingly followed his every direction.

I remember spending a lot of time gritting my teeth that winter and reminding myself that I loved my son and I would do anything to secure his happiness.

Belle spent a lot of time looking smug.

By the time the following spring rolled around an important decision had been made regarding our family and myself, my son and Belle found ourselves preparing to move to a small island off the west coast of Scotland. It was decided our older dogs would remain with his father, but there was no doubt where Belle would be going. We made the drive to our new home overnight and Belle behaved impeccably all the way up, albeit refusing to pee for more than thirteen hours.

We were all tense, nervous and very emotional and for the first time I began to see Belle other than the unfortunate birthday gift that kept on giving. When my son's father left us at our new home and returned to England my son was, understandably, distraught. I was drowning in guilt and nerves at the huge leap I'd taken in moving to a new country where we knew literally no one but each other and it was a terrifying few moments.

I remember looking down on the floor from where I lay on the bed, holding my crying son in my arms and meeting Belle's eyes. She looked back at me for a few moments and then jumped up onto the bed, climbed over my son to wriggle in between us and gave us both a series of sloppy licks over our wet faces. Logically I know that she was probably attracted to the salt from the tears, but I also like to think that she knew how frightened and desolate we were and that was her way of telling us that everything would be okay, she had it all under control.

And she did.

Belle came into her own with our move. The most important thing about her breed that I didn't understand was that Staffies need to be needed. What I had put down to ambivalence in her feelings to me in the beginning was actually her perception that I didn't need her. In her eyes, right from the start, my son did. He needed her love, her protection and her time and attention. I did not.

I had other dogs, other people and other things that took up my time and she took that to mean that she could ignore me. Moving away from everything we knew and, in effect, isolating ourselves changed her in ways I would never have believed possible at the beginning. She started to greet me when I came home from work, cuddle with me at night (although never when her first love was available) and slowly but surely we started to bond. What really cemented our new relationship was when my son visited his father and step-mother for a month over the summer and we were both suddenly bereft of the most important person in our lives.

We were both pining and lost without him for those four weeks, still adjusting to our new rural life after living in a town, and I don't know what I would have done without her for that time. She even, grudgingly, gave into her daily walks with something approaching good grace. When my son came home there was a different dynamic to our little family unit that had not been there before. We moved to permanent housing a few months after our relocation and that began one of the happiest times of Belle's life. My son had made some good friends at school but was still too young to be out at night so our flat was regularly filled with five or six extra boys that were filled with exuberance and, more importantly, were more than happy to give Belle all the attention she desired and, on occasion, crisps.

She always seemed to know when the weekend had rolled around. There was an extra spark in her eyes and her whole body was aquiver with anticipation. More often than not sleepovers had been arranged and she was practically coming apart at the seams with excitement by the time the last boy had come through the door, rucksack of fizzy drinks and junk food heavy on their shoulders. I generally would receive shouted hellos and then the whole mob of them, Belle firmly in the midst, would disappear into the bedroom, the door would slam shut and the party would go on to the wee hours as they got high on E numbers and preservatives. She was cuddled, she play fought, she was fed so much rubbish she looked like a little football with legs in the morning but she loved those boys with everything she had. I used to peep in on them on occasion and she would be making the rounds, cuddling each in turn, never leaving a soul out.

With the change in her personality I began to be concerned that she was becoming lonely at home on her own whilst I was at work and the child was at school. We had become good friends with some neighbours that owned a Staffie cross called Red and he lived in domestic bliss with a little cat called Shadow. I didn't feel it would be feasible to get another dog in a first floor flat, but I thought I could probably handle a house cat. Despite loathing – and being a little afraid of if I'm honest – cats all my life, I convinced myself I could get over this if I had a cat from a young age and got to know it as it grew up. I mentioned this in an aside to one of our neighbours and not 48 hours later she was on the phone to tell me she'd heard about some kittens and had reserved one for me, I could pick it up in four weeks.

I was thrilled.

The next four weeks were a rollercoaster ride of buyer's remorse, conviction that Belle would tear it to shreds the moment she saw it and desperately trying to think of a way to back out of the deal without offending my friend. However, my normally breath taking aptitude for weaselling out of things I didn't want to do failed me and four weeks later I found myself in a car on my way to collect the kitten, who we named Tee.

I now have five cats, just to reassure you. The story ends well and not with a helpless kitten being booted out into the snow.

Tee's father was a feral cat who had managed to surprise his mother one night while she was out for an innocent stroll and left her with rather more than she bargained for after their feline knee trembler. He wasn't especially friendly but he didn't seem overly averse to being handled either so we collected him and brought him back home to meet Belle.

It became apparent from the first meeting that only one of them was in charge and it wasn't the dog. She was delighted with the kitten and approached him gently with a wagging tail and a doe eyed expression on her face....and backed up smartly two seconds later when he hissed aggressively and swiped at her, narrowly avoiding taking out said doe eyes. Although it had become apparent in the time we had her that Belle was one of life's nurturers, she was not one of life's disciplinarians. She was desperate to love the kitten but Tee remained firmly convinced she wanted to eat him and so was resolutely on the defensive for the next few months.

Every time Belle went near him, even to innocently cross his path on her way somewhere else, he became a hissing, malevolent ball of teeth and claws and it was only through prolonged ignoring of him and, occasionally, shutting him in the bathroom out of sheer desperation that he finally calmed down. When he eventually decided that she posed no danger the change happened literally overnight and it was with a sense of relief that we slid into summer and Belle and Tee into a close friendship that persists to this day. They cuddled together, she licked him lovingly to sleep, he kneaded her head and bit her ears and she occasionally protected Brain the hamster when Tee decided to have another crack at breaking into his cage and eating him.

It was a golden summer.

We continued in this vein for another year and a half and Belle continued to grow into her role as the heart of the house. Her personality seemed to be ever expanding and there always seemed to be something new that she had learnt or taught herself. One of her most enduring habits was developed early on where she learnt that if she looked out the window in the morning before her walk then what was happening outside had a direct impact on how comfortable she would be when she went out. If she saw the rain coming down then it would be a battle of wits between us as she sought a safe hiding place and I tried to find her and get her lead on. One of her favourite tricks was to reverse around the flat, ducking her head as she tried to avoid having her harness fitted and grunting her displeasure at what was to happen. More often than not I'd be helpless with frustrated laughter as I battled with her and was often horrendously late for work just because my dog hated getting wet.

One Christmas I was talked into taking another kitten that was having difficulty finding a home for a trial of a week over the holiday period and, naturally, Greebo never left. Unlike Tee, Greebo was never aggressive but he was, and remains, the most incredibly shy cat I've ever come across. To this day there are a lot of people that don't believe he exists as he'll habitually show himself if it's only me around. He fitted seamlessly into the flat, mainly because we never saw him, but I decided that with three animals it was unfair to keep them in a home without outside access so we moved a few yards down the road to a house with a garden. Aside from Greebo getting hit by a car and having to be kept on cage rest for the following four months, this worked out very well and all the animals appreciated having their horizons expanded. One of Belle's favourite past times became sitting in the front window which looked directly onto the street and watching all the children walking home from school until she saw her boy pass by. Even though it's now years redundant she'll still wake up around three thirty and sit patiently in the front window of the house we live in now and watch for my son to come home.

Having successfully reared two kittens that were now fully grown cats and spent quite a bit of time out of the house Belle was in need of another project and my friend that had found my first kitten once more helped us out and informed us of some puppies that were in dire need of a home.

I use the words 'helped us out' in the loosest possible sense here.

Dally was, and remains, a special case. He came to our attention because he and his siblings had been dumped in a bucket in a town over on the mainland…and for good reason as it turns out. He had been born the runt of his litter and it was originally thought that he was nearly completely blind. He had been returned to the animal shelter that had originally taken him and, along with two of his sisters who were also thought to be partially sighted, was considered unlikely to be adopted and was probably going to be put to sleep. To this day I'm not sure what happened but a week later I found myself on a ferry with my friend to collect the three dogs as she rehomed the sisters and I rehomed Dally.

There was, and still is, nothing wrong with Dally's eyesight. He has vision like a hawk. What he does *not* have is brains. He is loving, joyful, enthusiastic and an eternal puppy, but he is not trainable. It has become evident that there is probably some neurological damage that manifests in some awkward physical movements and an almost pathological ineptitude to retain anything past basic training. He is house trained, he doesn't bite and he isn't destructive and that's as good as it gets with Dally. Basic commands are beyond him and with his arrival Belle's personality began to change once more.

One of the things that I'd always been most proud of about Belle was that she had never been defensive or aggressive with other dogs. She welcomed each one she met and had never so much as curled a lip at any dog we met, regardless of the other dog's behaviour. With Dally on the scene that began to change. Suddenly threats were everywhere. Any dog that approached would be greeted with ferocious barking and snarling and she would become almost manic in her need to protect her pup.

Dally remained oblivious to this and continued to joyfully make friends with whatever dog he met whilst his adoptive mother did her level best to eat them.

Belle became the stereotypical Staff for a while, to the point where I never took her outside without a muzzle in case she slipped her lead and went for another dog, but eventually reason returned. I knew why she was displaying this behaviour I just needed to find a way to deal with it. After some trial and error a workable system was put in place and implemented. Employing Belle's enduring love for anything edible I began to distract her with dog treats whenever another dog approached. Instead of turning and marching the other way when another dog appeared on the horizon, I kept moving on and Belle walking forward. Staffies also interpret body language in different ways to other dogs so I increased her doggy social circle and also asked unfamiliar dog owners if they would allow their dog to stand for a moment and be introduced to Belle so she could start to properly distinguish again between non-threatening and threatening behaviour. It remains a work in progress but the important thing about Belle is that she never forgets once she's been introduced to a dog and there is never a problem again between them if they meet. She also never forgets if a person has been kind to her, which generally equates to having been given food by someone. She will make a beeline for someone out walking, even if I barely remember them, and greet them like she saw them yesterday.

Fortunately being hit a knee level by an ecstatic dog who is expecting a dog biscuit forthwith is something that no one has taken offense to so far.

We moved again shortly after Greebo's accident to a house in a more remote location, far removed from any traffic and acquired what I thought would be our last kitten. Ferdy bonded immediately with Dally and would lay for hours suckling his teeth and kneading his muzzle in an apparent bid for milk. By far the most confident of all our older boys he inserted himself into the household and became an unholy terror for the next two years. He bullied Greebo, delighted in jumping out at Tee and scaring the living delights out of him and, distressingly, learnt to hunt at a very early age. He started small but soon graduated to bringing home rabbits the same size as himself and I was horrified to learn that there was a possibility of a woman who owned peacocks moving to the house behind us at one point. Visions of my small tabby cat dragging home colourful fowl dominated my thoughts for a few weeks before it was confirmed she would not be moving after all.

Through all this Belle remained her usual self, watching over her brood with love and care and displaying absolutely no inclination to assert herself in the pack to anything approaching a disciplinarian.

No matter how roughly they played or tormented her, she would lie on the floor and stare patiently into space as she was tugged around and give them the occasional lick to reassure them she still loved them. Another thing that has never changed has been her devotion to my son. He remains the great love of her life and it was with great reluctance that she has gradually come to accept that there is now another great love of his.

He'd brought home one girlfriend in his early adolescence but it was when he brought home his current one that Belle's life changed again. She seemed to know immediately that this one was different from the other people he had brought home and, in a way that only Belle could, made her feelings known. I would like to state for the record that the girlfriend is wonderful. I absolutely adore her and have welcomed her with open arms.

Belle? Not so much.

Right from the word go Belle refused to greet her when she came through the door. There was never any aggression, not so much as a curled lip, but she would take herself off to the other side of the room and turn her back and stare fixedly at the floor or wall, refusing to even turn her head let alone acknowledge the poor girl's presence.

Tempting her with treats didn't work. Talking to her, trying to sit next to her, whatever was tried was politely ignored.

Dally, on the other hand, thought the girlfriend was the best thing since sliced bread and was pretty much glued to her from the minute she walked in to the minute she left.

After a few months, when Belle eventually realised her passive resistance was failing, she devised a new method of trying to dispose of the interloper. She would wait for them to sit on the couch, possibly start to snuggle, and then would get onto the sofa, get between them and turn her back on the girlfriend and then push back with everything she had until the incredibly patient girlfriend was squashed into the corner and she was staring lovingly into my son's eyes once more. It got slightly rockier when the girlfriend started to stay over and Belle was displaced from her spot on the son's bed but they seem to have put it behind them and have reached a mutual accord.

Incredibly she managed to keep this up for nearly three years before she finally gave in and resigned herself to the fact that the girlfriend was here to stay.

These days they get on incredibly well and Belle is a big fan, largely due to the fact that now my son is at university she only sees the girlfriend when he comes home and so she now associates her with Good Things Happening.

There is no doubt she misses her boy and she pines dreadfully for him the first couple of days when he leaves after a visit. No matter how our relationship has changed, or what other distractions she has, Belle's true love will always remain my son. She knows when I open up his room and make the bed that he's close. I try to leave the preparations to the last possible moment these days as she will literally roam the house for hours, barking at every sound and crying desperately on his bed with excitement as she waits for him. The moment of reunion never fails to make me a little misty eyed. It's like his school days all over again. She flings herself into his waiting arms and grunts and huffs her excitement, anxiously smelling him and swiping her tongue over every patch of skin she can reach and soaking up his attention like a hyperactive sponge.

Some more recent additions to the household have helped alleviate her pining and it's fair to say that she's almost as besotted with them as she is with my son. I've recently homed two kittens from Romania who have one eye between them. They're slightly undersized, never roam but, more importantly, they are always going to need Belle. Roman is completely eyeless and his sister has custody of the lone eye and they worship their new mum as much as she loves them.

From the first introduction Belle knew that they were different from the other members of the household and for the first time ever she has started to put her other boys in their place if she feels her little ones are being tormented. Ferdy does not like the kittens and hisses and yowls at them on a regular basis so it's not uncommon to see Belle running between them and giving a sharp bark of disapproval to let him know this is not okay. Ferdy was so stunned the first time this happened that he flew out the back door in fright and didn't come back for four hours. Belle picked up Roman and took him to her bed for an extensive licking to help him get over the shock.

Another common sight is Belle trotting out into the back garden, closely followed in single file by the kittens, and supervising playtime outside. She's decided without me telling her that they are not allowed to roam as the three older cats are and will, quite literally, herd cats until they decide they've played enough and want to come in. Evenings will find us generally on the sofa, Belle on my legs and the kittens piled on top while occasionally Greebo and Dally are snuggled up against us and enjoying cuddle time.

She's not a perfect dog, not by any stretch of the imagination. As stated, she can be problematic if she thinks one of her brood is being threatened. She's a dreadful scrounger and she's never met a sausage she doesn't like. She has the rather upsetting habit of eating poo when on her walks and she *still* hates exercise and will do anything she can to avoid it – her favourite hiding place of the moment is under my son's old double bed where she scuttles and wedges herself into the furthest corner so that I have to commando crawl after her and pull her out by her front paws, chuntering angrily at me the whole time.

So Belle is not perfect, but what she is to us could never be quantified. Despite having pets my whole life I never understood the difference between 'pet' and 'companion' until Belle came to us. I love Dally very much, but in my heart of hearts he is a pet. Belle is so much more to me. She has been a comfort, a friend, a co-parent, a caregiver and so many other roles that I never would have believed an animal could be. She's been there when we went through the first experiments with alcohol (she even stayed at my son's side when he managed to miss the bucket and throw up over her instead), broken hearts, when I've had to be the disciplinarian but I couldn't be the comforter afterwards and she's been there when everything gets just a little too much and I just need someone to hug that won't judge where I am and choices I've made.

Any breed of dog can provide all that and more but what I didn't understand until I met Belle and what many people still fail to understand is that Staffies can, and do, provide that too. Almost invariably when you see a report on dangerous dogs or a documentary on TV Staffies are habitually used to illustrate the potential hazards of housing a dog. They are also invariably shown straining at the end of a leash, frothing at the mouth or running around uncontrollably, ignoring the commands of their impoverished owners. Unfair media representation and irresponsible reporting have contributed extremely negatively to the perception of Staffies and have also contributed to the high number of the breed being surrendered to shelters or being destroyed as they are found to be not suitable for the purpose they have been taken for, fighting or security, or people are not taking the time and trouble to properly care and train their dog.

Like any soul with a sense of identity, dogs have their own quirks. Belle's are not because she is a dog but because she is an *individual*. Do you like every person you meet and interact with them without a qualm? Then why should we expect the same of our canine companions? Belle is a part of our family and, as such, when her personality evolved we accommodated it and worked through it. If everyone who sees her and automatically puts her in the Staffie 'box' could come home with us and see her with her kittens or stoically sitting whilst a friend's new puppy yanks on her ears then I could guarantee they would never judge solely on its breed again.

She's funny, loyal, a little bit bi-polar and when the time comes for her to pass from the earth then, much like Marley of 'Marley & Me' fame, her epitaph can only be a few words – Belle: A Good Dog.

The next time you find yourself in a position of looking for a new animal to bring into your home please do yourselves a favour and go to your local shelter and look at their Staffies. I promise you that there will be plenty to choose from and, with proper love and care, you will never regret it.

Tiris Storyteller

By

Yvonnne Marjot

Excerpts from the novel '*Fire Under the Skin*'

'Fire Under the Skin' is a narrative told from the perspective of three people, each of whom has grown up in a different part of a nation divided and impoverished in the aftermath of a global catastrophe. Each has a role to play to ensure the future survival of the human community. Garand has lived a long and eventful life, and has chosen to settle in a desolate semi-urban community on the edge of a radioactive city. Rona was born and raised in the Sisterhood, a community of women almost completely isolated from the outside world. Tiris is the child of a rigid, fundamentalist community with no capacity for imagination or growth. These extracts tell the beginning of her story.

Cully's my pride and joy, my heart and soul, my best beloved, my one and only. My father laughed to hear the string of endearments as I lay on the mat and curled around my wee lad. Then his face turned solemn. 'Don't get attached, Tiris,' he said. 'He isn't going to live.'

I folded Cully's little ears over so that he wouldn't have to hear. Yes, he was the runt of the litter. Yes, his eyes were gummy and his ribs were sticking out and he had a puncture wound in his shoulder where one of his litter mates had attacked him, but none of that mattered. He was mine now, and this baby was going to live. He had to.

Pet dogs are unusual in our society. There are pig dogs, trained by hunters to help with the task of taking wild meat to supplement our diet. There are sheepdogs – fleet and intelligent, they are bred and trained by those with the Mastery of shepherding, and can only be owned by shepherd families. Some wealthy women have lap dogs – little, yapping rats that can fit in a handbag, which live the cosseted lives of babies that never grow up. And there are mongrel packs hanging around the edge of every town – alert to any scrap that may come their way.

The wild dogs are taboo. Children are taught not to approach them. This is partly because they eat what is dead and discarded, and are regarded as unclean. But every child is warned that the dog packs will eat a living child, if they cannot get a dead one. They are creatures of nightmare, and none of us would dream of approaching them.

Cully was something different. His mother had been brought to town by a pedlar, an itinerant trader of threads, buttons and whatnots, whose skill at wood-turning adorned many a wealthy household in the town. It was said that the Teacher's husband had a complete chess set carved by him. At his side strode a black and tan bitch whose head stood as high as his waist, and whose plumed tail wagged for joy at the sight of every stranger.

The pedlar is irresistible to children, because he comes from far away and everyone knows that means new stories. Of course, they are still permitted stories - nothing is really new under the sun - but we hadn't heard them since last he passed this way, and that was as good as a fair to a bored child.

"Gemmery! Gemmery's here." For a moment I was just like any other child in the group. We ran down the main street, giggling and shoving each other in our excitement. We stopped as he drew closer – none of us wanted to be the first to approach the unknown dog, but he spoke to her quietly, "Sit, Missie," and the dog settled to her haunches and watched us, tongue lolling.

Gemmery bent his legs and settled to the level of the smaller ones. "Hello, my pretties. Did you miss your Gemmery?" He pinched one red-haired toddler on her cheek and straightened, gesturing to us older ones, still hanging back. "Not got any new stories for your old friend?"

The little ones jumped and shouted. "Gannus has rabbits. They ate up all his garden." "Have you got ribbons? My Auntie wants a green ribbon." The smith's shed fell down." "My baby sister got born."

At this last, Gemmery turned to the boy who had spoken. "My respect to your mother," he said. "Is she well?" The boy nodded, solemn now. The birth of a child is a serious event, and often enough the child or the mother is harmed by it. It's never taken lightly.

He raised his eyes to us olders, standing at the back. Nikal Jons spoke. "What breed of dog is that. I don't recognise it."

Gemmery ignored the faint suggestion of threat. Acceptability of breed would not be decided by adolescents, no matter how highly born (and Nikal was only the son of a tailor).

"Missie? She's a Gemmeran Shepherd. My wife got her for me, to guard me on my travels. She liked the name." His face quirked in a smile. "It's a common enough breed up the coast. Shepherds cross them with their working dogs to get more strength in the breed. They're good with animals, and good for guarding. Nice dogs with people, too. Maritun approved them, about five years ago."

Nikal's hackles settled. Maritun was a large place, reputed to be full of strange folk with strange ideas, but still a town of the people. Gemmery's answer was a good one, and likely to sit well with the elders if required.

The old man's gaze ranged over the assembled children again. His glance fell on me, and paused for a moment, but he passed on. He knew well I would be there for every story, every account of his journeys, every cautionary tale. Once I'd given in to temptation and told him one of my own stories, as he packed his possessions carefully to take on to the next town. He'd listened all right, without comment, but afterwards he stopped his work and took my hands. "Tiris, where did you hear that story?"

"Nowhere. I made it up myself."

His face was kind, and troubled. "And who have you told it to?"

"Only my mother."

"What did she say?"

"She told me not to tell it to anyone else."

"She's right. It's not safe to tell your own stories."

"You do."

"Oh no, little one. The stories I tell are age-old and sanctioned by authority. The Teacher herself could listen to my tales and be undisturbed. Don't you know – all stories are part of the Teaching? No-one may invent their own."

"Somebody has to make up new stories." I still didn't understand. I was full of stories, wanting to tell themselves. Surely there must be a Mastery with room for that?

"Perhaps the teachers may. I wouldn't know. I only tell the stories I'm allowed to tell. Even a pedlar has his Questions and Answers, you know."

I'd left him, still confused and unrepentant, but a week later I'd made the mistake of beginning to tell the story to my father. He too had recognised it for something new – and the resultant beating left me too sore to sit down for a week.

Gemmery's eye met mine again and I dropped my gaze. Perhaps there would be a time to talk to him later. Perhaps. Although I was beginning to understand that my stories needed to stay shut up inside my head, at least until I succeeded in gaining the teaching apprenticeship I was aiming for.

Missie turned out to be pregnant, and a few weeks later the eagerly awaited puppies arrived to an attendant audience of children. The first two pups were fat and squirmed deliciously in our outstretched hands, but the third was a runt, scrawny and undersized. After the third pup, the bitch strained and pushed for hours, gradually becoming exhausted, and at last delivered herself of a dead puppy. After that, she lay exhausted and ill for many days.

The pups suckled eagerly at her flanks, and she roused herself to nose and lick them from time to time, but the pedlar was very worried about her. He watched over her, and fed her from his own plate, and gradually she improved. He said he'd been worried she had a dead pup stuck inside her, and could have died of it, but after a time he concluded that she had just been exhausted by the process of birth.

The fat puppies grew apace, and the children fought over who was to have them. Pointless fighting. The Teacher's son got the female, and the Master Shepherd the male, to be used for improving their inbred collie stock. No-one wanted the runt. It had a sore along its jaw line and a notch out of one ear, where the other pups had bitten it, and it lay, thin and listless, at its mother's side, hardly able to summon the energy to fight its siblings for a place at the teat. It seemed odd that, with only three puppies, the runt could not have ready access to the nipple, but the pedlar explained that this was normal for dogs. If the runt can't complete with its littermates, then it doesn't deserve to survive.

I couldn't bear the sight of the tiny body, panting, all its ribs showing. I'd shoulder aside the bigger pups and press the wee body against the mother's teats until it latched on. It could suck all right – it had the instinct to live; it was only that its brother and sister were so much bigger, so much more dominant. I began to plead with the pedlar to give the pup to me. I was sure that this time I wouldn't allow the baby to die.

The man was ready to move on, his bitch back on her feet and the older pups homed. He let me put the runt to the nipple one last time, then lifted it and shoved it into my arms. Without a word, he turned away and the bitch followed him. With the puppy tucked inside my shirt I ran home, hunched round his skinny body, trembling with fear and excitement.

At first I fed him from my own plate, but father said that what was right for me was not right for a dog, so I had to do extra chores to earn the right to claim food for him. I cooked the meat myself and chewed it, so that his poor sore jaw would not have to cope with breaking down the stringy gristle and protein. I fed him boiled water and cooked vegetables that were soft and easy to swallow. I slept on his mat every night, my body curled around his as if we were puppies together.

He soiled himself, too, and I had to clear the mess and clean him. Father was probably right - a sickly puppy separated from his dam would normally die - but I was determined to prove him wrong, and I did.

My dog not only survived and grew: he thrived on the attention I gave him. Within a week he was sitting up and following my every move with his eyes. As soon as his eyes brightened and his demeanour became more responsive, I began to train him. 'It's too soon,' they all said. 'It's a runt. What is the point of training it? What use will it ever be?' Even father thought it. I saw it in his eyes, although he was too kind to voice his opinion.

Eighteen months later I had a good dog, strong and healthy, alert and bright and completely attentive to my command. He would behave for father, too. He knew what was expected of him, although he wasn't above sneaking food or chewing one of the boys' shoes if he thought no-one was watching. He understood when he did wrong: I would hear the students shouting at home, or my father's gruff voice, and I would run in to find Cully lying on the floor with his paws over his face (if you can't see me then you can't tell me off). Then I would have to administer the discipline.

He was my dog; his behaviour reflected on me. It didn't take Cully long to learn that he was to obey me, and to perform as I expected, whether I was there or not. He was smarter than most people that way.

He was my partner when I undertook the plan to make my father approve of me. Father had already taught me a lot; more than most young ones, and probably more than most girls of any age. He'd been married to a Brewster, and even I knew that it was rarer for women to achieve full Mastery than men. It simply took too much effort, when having babies and deferring to the Master in your home was so much easier. I already knew girls whose only ambition was to learn enough of the crafts of home and hearth to attract a good husband, one whose Mastery carried prestige that they could acquire at second hand. Not me. I wanted Mastery of my own. Most of all, I wanted knowledge.

The students were already used to me following them around. It was easy to eavesdrop when they were practicing their catechisms and going through the rote parts of the Mastery lessons. A tutor teaches boys from about ten to fourteen, from the time they leave school until they come of age and apprentice for their Mastery. He helps them to learn which skills are most suited to them, and helps each to learn the catechetics that belong to the disciplines which interest them. These question-and-answer sequences are one of the main ways that a Master will use to decide which of a number of potential apprentices shows the most promise.

At eight, I'd exhausted all the domestic knowledge my parents and the household servants could teach me. I was still hungry for more. I think Father let me sit in with his students to keep me from getting into any more trouble elsewhere.

It was easy to pick up the catechetics for every subject my father taught. It was harder work comprehending the exercises. It wasn't enough to learn by heart; I wanted to understand each subject as I learned it. I wanted to be able to show my father that I understood all of them as well as he did.

Each day I climbed the apple tree at the bottom of the garden and sat looking out over the wall to the far hills. Cully would wait patiently at the base of the tree while I sorted out the new learning in my head, and recited the latest set of Answers I had learned. After a while my droning voice bored him and he would settle, paws over his eyes, and sleep as I talked on.

He sat by my side for hours as I drew diagrams and solved equations in the dust. I could have stolen paper and charcoal - even with the great care my father took not to waste resources, there were always spoiled exercises and crumpled workings to be rescued from the kindling basket - but I kept those for my stories. I didn't want to leave any evidence of my studies. When I revealed my learning to my father, I wanted it to be a surprise.

...

My father was the senior tutor. It really wasn't his fault. With older boys in and out of his house, day and night, studying with him and learning the Arcana, such that are left to us, he had little enough time for a girl child under his feet. I adored him. I would have done anything to get his attention, but I was always in the way. He was forever brushing me aside, saying 'Later, child,' as if 'later' meant anything different than 'never.' It wasn't his fault that I realised at last the one thing that would make him notice me.

Mother was different. My earliest memory is the brush against me of her long hessian apron, the mark of her Mastery, and the yeasty smell of hops and barley fermenting. Those, and a low, calm voice. She didn't have much to do with the boring business of child-raising. Being in a two-Mastery household meant that we had servants to do much of the work, and the job of changing my dirty small-clothes and drying my baby tears fell to a series of nannies and nursemaids. But I only need to think of Mother and I hear again that low voice, murmuring.

She never raised that voice against my father, never indulged in anger or recrimination. Her long battle with him was like that of the land against the sea, endlessly resisting its ceaseless argument. She was quietly proud of her Mastery, and would never give it up, even though Father argued that having a second working parent lowered the visible status of our household. People were saying that he couldn't afford to keep his wife. That she had to work. He understood that she was a Brewster, but she'd already proved herself. There was no need for her to work any longer. And so on, and so forth. It was his eternal litany.

On high days and holidays she would dress in silks and embroidered kirtle, to attend Teaching sessions or meetings of the Council, demure at my father's side. I disliked the necessity of sitting still, and the starched collars and itchy stockings I had to wear, but I was proud of my tall, elegant father and his handsome wife. Still, I couldn't imagine her becoming the kind of woman who sat out her days in the front parlour, knitting stockings or embroidering bedclothes. She'd be the first to say that, Mastery aside, she had no skills in the household arts.

Some looked askance at us, walking through the marketplace. I was quite young when I first became aware that it was unusual for a woman of my mother's status to continue to work after marriage. In theory men and women are all workers, all serve apprenticeship, all attempt Mastery; in practice the girl children of wealthy households are not expected to excel. A man is judged by his peers, and perhaps more pointedly by his wife's peers, on the basis of how well he can support his family on his own earnings. The idleness of wealthy women is a mark of status.

Mama had no time for that. She was proud of her Mastery, and frequently reminded us that the fame of our town's beer was due to her skill. "You need never be ashamed of my work," she would say, laying her hand on his cheek and smiling up at him. "We take status from each other."

That wasn't her only sign of rebellion. The memories I cherish more than any others are the stories she told me – strange products of her imagination, nothing like the reality of our lives. Sometimes she said they were dreams, and sometimes memories: memories of things that have never been nor could ever be. When I pressed her she would laugh and hug me. "When the mind is not used," she would say, "it feeds itself on stories. When you're older, you'll see what I mean. But don't go sharing them. Imagination is all very well between these four walls, but you're not to take our stories to the world. They aren't for sharing."

That piece of advice I failed to take to heart. I lived to regret it.

Father said that was where I'd got my stories: from her tellings. That even though I said I didn't remember her words, they must have all gone into my ears and stuck there, only to make their way out years later when I was supposed to be using the charcoal and precious paper for sums, or catechisms, or reminding myself of the rules of Mastery.

I would come home from school with my palm red and stinging from the cane, clutching a crumpled up piece of paper in my other hand – a paper on which were written tens, dozens, hundreds of words working together to make a pattern that linked my mind and my voice and my writing hand and told a story. A story, in a place where only fact had value, and imagination was a threat to all. A story: no longer legible for the smudging of a great palm across its centre, and five huge letters in black: WASTE.

For waste my father would paddle me, and I would cry, for form's sake, although the layers of my skirts protected me from the sting of the paddle and, anyway, I didn't care if it hurt. The sting of my palm was more painful, and the worst pain of all was the loss of the story.

Then he would sit me down and try to explain, again, why it was so important for me to demonstrate that I knew and understood the catechisms, and the prescribed forms of learning, and why I mustn't allow my mind to wander into the realms of imagination, or my fingers to wander, clutching the charcoal, across the page, turning the images in my mind into words on the paper that could put images into other people's minds.

It was very important that I not trespass on the Teacher's Mastery. If at coming-of-age I was chosen to be a teacher, I could look forward to many more years of apprenticeship, working with my father and with the Teacher or others of her profession, until I knew all the

Arcana for all the Masteries, and could pass them on as required to the apprentices in my classes. But even after achieving Mastery, a teacher does not look for new stories to tell.

It could take a lifetime to learn all the prescribed stories and traditional parables. There was no need for anything new. And certainly no need for a child who has not even come of age to be thinking up new things, when there is so much still to be learned.

I would nod, and snivel, and promise. Anything to stop my father being angry at me. Anything to make the lesson end, so that I could be allowed to go to my bed and 'think about what you have done.' And then I would lie in the darkness, free from scrutiny, and close my eyes to see great beasts cavorting in the waters of the sea, great machines grinding up the deep treasures of the earth, great roaring birds larger than houses leaping into the air and crossing oceans - none of which existed, or had ever existed, outside my ridiculous imagination - while all the time the fingers of my writing hand twitched and curled, writing out the stories as I lived them in the tight, red darkness behind my squeezed shut eyes.

...

This task I've set myself – it's hard. It's not just my story. I need to tell the Story of Three (although I grieve with all my heart that it's no longer the Story of Four). Even then, though, it's much more than that. It's everyone's story. It's so hard to know where to start. I think back to the best advisers of my childhood.

My mother would have told me to have faith in myself. But she would also have warned me not to tell the story. 'Keep your stories inside your head', she said. 'You don't understand how dangerous it is to share them'.

Father's advice would have been even more straightforward. 'Take each Question in its own place. Learn the Answer. Once you are word perfect, move on. But take my advice, Tiris. Listen to me. Don't make up your own words. You must learn the Answers exactly as I teach them to you. Only the Answer is right. You may not tell it in your own way.'

Oh, it's no use. There are no Answers for what I need to write, and there are too many Questions, all nebulous and ill-formed. There doesn't seem to be any order or reason to what happened. It just did, and now I need to write about it, There are so many places where I could start. I think back to my youngest years, when words came tripping off my tongue faster than I could say them, and Mama knew just what advice to give me.

'Start at the beginning, Tiris. Start at the beginning, and go on until you reach the end.'

...

'Tiris Mattier, get away from my apples!'

Robbo and I scrambled for the wall. My friend was faster than me, and shot over like an arrow from a crossbow. I was only just behind him, but inevitably I was the one to get spotted. A windfall hit me on the back of the head, catapulting me over the broken edge of the wall and down into the ditch on the other side. The irate shout followed us. 'Just wait till I talk to your father about this.'

I sat in the ditch, trousers soaked with muddy water, and felt my head. A lump was coming up, tender to the touch, and the fermented juice of the windfall clotted my hair and dribbled down the back of my neck. At least, I thought it was apple juice. I brought my hand round to my mouth and licked it. Yeah, apple juice. At least it wasn't blood. Robbo was off, running scared. I could see his head bobbing between the sapling trees of the new plantation as he headed down the track.

'Hey,' I shouted. 'Robbo, watch it. You're losing them.' Behind the fleeing figure was a growing trail of fruit. He must have had two dozen stuffed up his shirt, but those he hadn't lost on his flight from the orchard were falling one by one as he ran in panic. 'Robbo!'

He wasn't listening, too busy saving his own skin. I stood up and checked my own haul – the front of my jersey was stretched out of shape with my share of contraband. I began to make my own way home, picking up the dropped apples as I went. There wasn't any point in running. The farmer knew exactly who I was. If he hadn't recognised me, he'd be bound to have noticed the pup, now half-grown, trotting at heel as I sauntered away.

...

I finished my basic schooling in my eleventh year. There followed one year when I worked at the feet of the apprentices in several Masteries. This gives youngsters the chance to experience some real work, and to gain some idea of the Mastery that each may wish to pursue. Some parents purchase immunity from such work for their children, but my father did not. I was glad of it: by working hard and keeping my mouth shut I learned a lot about how our society functioned. Not that I found it easy to keep quiet – it was the potter's fist that taught me, finally, that he did not appreciate my chatter and would not answer my questions.

A lot of the work was difficult. Not that it was hard to understand; I listened avidly as the apprentices were shown their tasks, and did my best to emulate their efforts without direct teaching, but, to be honest, I didn't get much chance to show my worth.

I was set to cutting standard sized lumps of clay, ready for the potter, and to constantly cleaning and refilling the buckets of water used in the pottery process. I was too small to be trusted with the wood-chopping axe, but I could be set to trudge backwards and forwards with armloads of fuel for the kilns, hour after hour.

In the smithy I was next to useless: neither strong enough nor tall enough to help with even the simplest of tasks. The smith, too, had a hard fist, but he didn't care about my talk. The smithy was so noisy, and his concentration so intense, that I could chatter on for hours, perched safely out of the way, and he took little notice. His apprentices were both older boys, tall and broad in the shoulder. I admired them, but they had not much in the way of conversation.

My favourite time was when I was sent out with the hunters. There were three of them looking to take on an apprentice in the next round, and they took three twelve-year-olds on a series of forced marches into the mountains. I thought it would be good to have company my own age, but it didn't turn out that way. One boy was a snivelling weed who tagged a few paces behind the rear of the group, and whined the whole time about being wet, or cold, or dirty. He balked, too, at being handed a knife and told to skin and gut the first possum. The other was quiet, reserved, no kind of company at all; though as happy as I was to try everything we were taught to do.

I found it fascinating to learn how best to gut a small animal without breaking the intestine and spoiling the meat, how to slice the skin down the belly, right through the fatty layer around the groin, and down the length of the limbs, and then carefully peel the pelt right off without damaging the fine fur. I learned how to cook possum stew, how best to trap moalings (I already knew how to pluck and prepare the plump birds for the pot, they were one of my Father's favourite meals), how to stalk the great antlered deer, and how to tell pig sign in order to avoid them. Wild pigs are dangerous.

I memorised the names of all the great peaks in the eastern range, which ran for hundreds of miles along the outer edge of our lands, and I learned the signs that marked out the routes to the two great passes that were the only known ways to cross the mountains to the coastal plains on the other side. Not that we went all the way. The hunters knew their territory well, but they were not explorers. What lay on the other side was only rumour to them, and they didn't bother to cross the range. Why hunt across the mountains, when there was plenty to be had closer to home?

Working with the broiderers was the most boring job. It wasn't that the work lacked interest, or variety; it was only that I didn't get the chance to experience any of it. Chat was not an issue - the older girls talked among themselves all the time - but when I attempted to contribute to the conversation they would all fall silent and stare at me with bright eyes, like so many birds. It didn't do any good to ask questions, either. When I asked why it was that I was set, day after day, to make so many rows of plain split stitch across the same piece of rough cloth, unpicking it each evening so as to start again the next day, I was told: 'because I tell you to.' And on asking what was the use of the split stitch, as opposed to satin stitch, or couching, or any of the more complex stitches the apprentices were learning, the answer was even less forthcoming: 'shut up and sew.'

I concluded that the primary purpose of the task was to teach me self-discipline, and set myself to endure it for the sake of practising that skill. The purpose of the chatter seemed to be gossip, and I gave up trying to worm myself into their conversations: there was not much for me to learn there.

Each evening I made my way home, sore and weary by turns in my back, arms, legs and fingers, to share the meal with my father and the students and to take Cully for his second walk. Afterwards, the students would settle themselves around the hearth and Father would fire questions at them - catechetics, mostly, but sometimes questions that required thought and calculation - and I would curl up in the corner, with Cully warming my feet, and answer along with them; silently, as I'd learned from Simeon Potter. In this way, although I was no longer able to listen in to lessons, I kept my hand in by hearing and memorising all the Questions and Answers.

At the end of my twelfth year I was ready for formal tutoring. Father took only male students, so I would have to go to the girls' tutor in the next village. I was lucky at that - many children see out a second year of work before they are presented for apprenticeship - but you are more likely to achieve Mastery if you have your year of tutoring.

The day came that the other girls of my year assembled in the marketplace, and climbed aboard a wagon for their first day's schooling. Father had said nothing to me, so I didn't go. I was pleased to have a holiday, and took Cully up into the hills to look for bees' nests. We came home mid-afternoon, filthy, swollen with stings and sticky with stolen honey. I left a comb of it for Father and took myself to the baths.

After a week of it I was not so sanguine. I knew that I had already learned everything Father had to teach me, so I had no fear that a week's holiday would spoil my education. It was only that I wondered whether the girls' tutor would have different things to teach. Different Questions and Answers. If there were Arcana that I hadn't learned yet, then now was the time to be doing it, before I turned fourteen and it was too late.

The week taught me something else as well. I came to understand that while I had been out on my work year, a woman had been coming round to see my father. Not in the evenings, when all the students were there, but after the midday meal, when the students were resting or away to the baths or the gym. I met her leaving as I arrived on the day of the bee stings.

"Hello, I'm Tiris Mattier."

She gave me the strangest look. I wondered if I was perhaps even dirtier than I'd thought; it was that which made me decide a bath was in order.

"Hello." She looked as though she was about to say more, but her face closed and she turned away and let herself out of the house. A strange encounter, though I didn't think any more about it at the time.

But she was there every afternoon of that week, privately closeted with Father, and she gave me the same peculiar look each day as she was leaving. Later, I understood what it meant, but at the time it was puzzling. Father didn't take female students, and although she was much younger that him she was certainly far too old for an apprentice.

I thought she might be a teacher; they are the only ones who carry on learning all through their teaching careers, because a teacher may be called upon to provide tutoring or advice in any walk of life, and it takes a lifetime to learn all the Answers. But when I asked Father he crinkled his eyes as if I'd said something amusing and didn't answer.

...

"Work it harder. Really put your back into it. Yes, that's better."

My mother's voice nattered on as I kneaded the dough, side by side with her at the kitchen table. We hardly ever made our own bread. Mama was the Master Brewster, so she worked all the time with the yeasts that are used to make beer. She couldn't work with bread yeasts, for fear of contaminating the brew, so most of the time we made do with a mix of drop scones, damper bread and unleavened bread pockets. Sometimes she sent me to the market, to barter for a loaf of good, yeast-risen bread. That was a rare treat, though.

This week she was on holiday, because the last batch of beer had been kegged and the vats needed to be washed. It's a specialist task – if the vats aren't thoroughly cleaned, then the new batch of beer could be soured by stale yeasts from the last brewing. Mama's precious yeast starter is clean, but the vats can harbour bacteria that feed on the beery residues, so they are regularly scrubbed. Mostly they only clean the vats, but this time it was the annual deep clean of the brewery complex and she was banned from the premises for a five-day.

In a corner of the kitchen we kept the brewer's yeast warm and comfortable. It was Mama's job to keep the starter alive until the brewery opened again. The starter is a living thing, though, and mustn't be ignored. The kitchen temperature and humidity had to be kept just right, the yeast must be fed – but not too much, or it bubbles up and overflows its container. Every now and again you have to skim some off, or it outgrows its pot.

When it does, we use the excess to make bread. Mama's beer bread is light but chewy, and it has a nutty, savoury taste. You'd think it would taste of beer, but it doesn't. It's the hops and malted barley that give the beer its flavour and sweetness. The yeast is just another variety of the organism that raises ordinary bread, but somehow it has a flavour all its own. Fresh out of the oven, broken open and drizzled with oil, it's still the best thing I've ever tasted.

I kneaded and rolled the dough fiercely, willing it to become smooth and silky, ready for its second rising. I couldn't wait to have that taste in my mouth.

My nose itched, and I rubbed it against the back of my arm. I glanced across at Mama and noticed that she had a smudge of flour across her face where she had done the same. She grinned at me, and bent again to her kneading. She had warm, brown eyes in a tired face, and her dark curls were tied back in a ponytail. She wore a patterned headscarf – another sign of her holiday. At work she wore a white hat, and her hair was always completely covered. She was very serious about her work.

Not all women practice their Mastery – these days it's fashionable to stay home and keep the house, and let the man's Mastery reflect on the whole household. Mama's proud of her brewing skills, though. There were some male brewers in our town, but the Master Maltster was also a woman: Mama's best friend, Kindsey. They made a formidable team.

"That's good, Tiris. Shape it now – think what size you want your loaf to be. You can probably make two loaves from your piece." She handed me the big knife and I cut my mound of dough into two pieces and shaped them into rough ovals with my hands. We laid out four pieces on a tray and she covered them with a cloth and put the tray in the warm corner next to the yeast keg. We washed our hands and faces at the outside tub: a little ritual of cleanliness, its familiar routine was comforting. She hung her apron up inside the door and took my hand.

"Walk with me, Tiris."

...

I came awake suddenly, eyes blinded by tears, clutching at the ground as if at my bedclothes at home. Cully lifted his head, instantly alert, all his senses seeking for the danger, trying to identify what had wakened me. But the fear and misery was all in my head. I had been so happy in that moment. I didn't want to remember what happened afterwards. I screwed my eyes shut, trying to shut out the memory, but it forced itself on me. I buried my face in Cully's side, breathing in the doggy smell of him, and clung onto his fur as the rest of it rose up in my mind and buried me. As I fell back into darkness I felt the rough warmth of his tongue on my hand, anchoring me to reality.

We walked together, my mother and I, down through the garden and out the small gate into the parkland that backed onto our street. It was a rare treat to spend time with her, and the warmth of the sun was an unlooked for pleasure.

"Tiris, I wanted you to be one of the first to know. I'm going to have a baby."

"Oh, Mama." I threw my arms around her and hugged her hard. She knelt down and held my shoulders.
"I'm going to need your help. This little brother or sister will be a precious new part of our family. You'll be the big sister. It's a big responsibility."

"I don't mind. What do I need to do?"

"There won't be much to do in the beginning. I have to remember to look after myself, to give this baby the best chance. I might need your help to prepare. We have to make some baby clothes, too. You can hem the nappets if you like.

"It's time for you to learn about babies and childbirth, now. One day, you will be married and if you are lucky you'll be able to have a child of your own. Not everyone can. It's very easy for the mother or the child to get sick, and then the baby is born dead, or the mother becomes ill. You have to eat the right food, and behave in the right way. There are some new Questions and Answers for you to learn now."

The baby was due early in the spring. The news made me very happy. There would be someone to share the child's burden, someone else to distract my parents. Someone new to play with. Understandably, I saw it mostly in terms of my own benefit.

Mama explained that having the baby would make her very tired, that she would need my help. I was full of plans to help her. It didn't work out that way.

Father was pleased, of course. It called for celebration. He took advantage of Mama's holiday from work to invite friends to visit, to hold at-homes for the neighbours, to parade her around the Council house and the town, smiling and complaisant on his arm. I felt shut out by these adult rites, but Mama took me to her each evening in the quiet of her parlour, and we talked about what a baby means, how it grows in the protection of the womb, what will happen at birth.

This process is not hidden in our community – it's a natural part of life, and we've all seen it with animals during childhood - but for the first time Mama spoke to me as a woman. I was excited to be told that one day it would be my part to bear a child for my family, and there was a lot to remember.

Babies don't just grow. They need to be nurtured. The woman must nourish herself both physically and emotionally if she wants to conceive. Not every woman will succeed. The man, too, must do his part to keep himself healthy, and to achieve a decent Mastery so that he can support his children. That was another opportunity for conflict between my parents, as looking back I see was only to be expected.

Father assumed that now she was pregnant my mother would give up work. Now, at last, she would have to accept that working at her Mastery was no longer appropriate. At some point during each evening of her holiday, he took the opportunity to press his case again. During the day they were united – presenting a happy, untroubled family face to the world. In private, he was relentless. She went back to work, of course, but the nagging didn't stop.

Each evening, when the working day was over, he would leave his students reciting their catechetics and come to the parlour to plead with Mama. She had to understand – he had a position to uphold. There was no need for her to work; he made more than enough to support all of us. Couldn't she see what she was doing to him?

The elders on the Council had been very kind, they had implied there might be a place among them for a tutor of his standing. He would very much like to enter political life - she knew he'd always had an interest - but a family where both adults worked? That really wasn't acceptable in polite society. She was being selfish. Wasn't it enough that he'd allowed her this second child, despite the risks? Did she have to throw his hard work back in his face? When was she going to accept that her Mastery was unimportant, that anyone could brew a drinkable keg of beer, it didn't have to be his wife? It just wasn't decent.

During the day, I kept out of his way, after the occasion when he cornered me in the corridor outside my room and badgered me to join him in trying to persuade Mama to 'see reason'. I loved my father, but I loved Mama too. I didn't see what was so wrong in her Mastery. We're all taught to work hard at what we do, and to do what we are best at, for the good of the community. I was too young to defend myself from his logic, and I didn't want to be the pummelling bag in the middle of their argument, so whenever I wasn't wanted for chores or classes, I took to climbing out my window and going out to the farms on the edge of town.

I learned a whole new set of Questions and Answers from the farm hands. Alec in the piggery was my favourite. I would stand on the middle bar of the gate as he scraped out the muck and straw, hosed down the yard and brought in fresh bedding for his beloved sows. He liked to talk, did Alec, and nothing pleased him more than a quiet, attentive listener. He had names for all his lasses, although he didn't name the piglets. No point, when they are going to die so young.

He explained the need to give each sow her own enclosure, so that she can bear her piglets in peace. The pens were designed to minimise the risk that the sow would roll over on top of her own young. That can happen.

...

A cold wind slithered into our shelter and half-woke me. I came to for a few minutes, my head pillowed on Cully's flank. We were off the bare mountainside, but barely under the meagre cover of stunted trees, and at such high altitude it was very cold out there. My dog and I needed each other – quite possibly, I'd have died in my first few weeks of exile without him. I turned my head back into the shelter of his body and let myself slip back into the memory. I couldn't hide from it under the reek of the piggery, any more than in the warm aroma of bread. It was time I let the memory run to its end. Time to revisit the moment that had changed my life forever.

It had seemed such an ordinary day. I'd completed my own catechetics with Father, done my chores, and gone out to pick over the frosted clods of the kitchen garden, searching deep into the bramble hedge for any left over, half dried blackberries, or chasing the chickens – such local domestic mischief as I could find, in this deep winter weather that kept me close to home.

A sudden kerfuffle of noise and activity in the kitchen drew my attention, and I slipped in through the half door to the warmth of the hearthside. Mama was home. That was entirely unexpected, for a work day, but more so was the air of panic among the other women of the household. Like the chickens I'd been chasing, they squawked and scattered. No-one was talking charge.

In the midst of it all my mother sat, legs apart, head hanging forward, on one of the hard kitchen chairs. Her hair was lank, wreathing her sweat-marked face, and she was panting, the hard, short breaths of an animal in pain. Most frightening, though, was a familiar stench in the wrong place: the hot, metallic smell of blood.

...

The smell of blood. It wasn't new. I'd been on the farm when they killed old layers for the pot. I'd peered into the slaughterhouse, where stripped carcasses hung on hooks ready for butchering. I'd skinned and gutted small animals during my hunt training. Blood was just part of animal life – part of eating – part of death. Nothing out of the ordinary.

Now, though, it held a different message. Blood in pools. Blood in spatters and patches, all over the place. Blood on the women of the household, working in silence as the situation steadily got worse. Blood on me, where I'd got in the way. Blood-stained cloths, and bloody water in pails, standing around on the floor, since no-one had the leisure to empty them, and in the heart of all that blood and silence, the grunting, writhing figure of my mother, panting in agony, the whites of her eyes showing all round the iris as she threw her head back in another contraction.

To begin with everyone had been reassuring. There was worry under the calmness, right enough. Even I knew that the baby was coming too soon. That wasn't good. But Mama had stroked my head and told me it was all going to be fine, and our housekeeper, bent between Mama's legs with bloodied cloths and a pail of warm water, told me to calm myself and go to fetch Mirna Midwife. She knew everything there was to know about childbirth. She'd be the one to bring my little brother or sister into the world, and give me back my mother.

Mirna Midwife had come. She sent for more help. She moved us into the bedroom, away from the bustle of the kitchen. She barred my father from the house when his questions had become too demanding. 'Your wife needs you to be calm and supportive. This energy is wrong. The mother and the child need calmness and peace. Be off with you. Seek your fellows – let them comfort you. You'll get none here.'

To my surprise, he'd gone without a word. Gone and left me here, in this room, which got redder by the minute.

I tried to make myself move. There were useful tasks I could be doing. Fetching clean water. Washing pails. Wringing out bloodied cloths and replacing them with clean ones from the laundry. But I couldn't tear my gaze from my mother's face.

She'd long since given up trying to work with the contractions. Her face was white, bloodless, as she hung in the women's arms, belly straining as if it had a life of its own, completely separate from the limp body and its dead eyes. I stared into those eyes, willing them to brighten with recognition, to see me, but she was long gone from this room, with its abattoir smell and coating of scarlet paint. She breathed - she lived - but she wasn't really here.

A moment later she roused herself, half rising on shaking thighs, and groaned, deep and protesting. As she bore down, something small and red eased itself into the midwife's hands. As Mirna looked down to see what had emerged from my mother's body, it was followed by a great gout of blood. Mama sagged, her eyes closing, and let go. Mirna half turned, thrusting the object behind her. 'Take this. I need to see to her.'

I jumped forward. I didn't intend to, but my body made its own decision. It had to. There was no one else. The women lowered my mother's unconscious body to the floor and began to work over it. I looked at the thing I held. It squirmed in my hands, and squealed softly. It jerked suddenly, as the cord came free, and Mirna looked round long enough to grasp the cut cord and fasten it with a peg. Then she turned back to her bloody work. I lifted the little body and held it against my chest. I could feel it gasping for breath.

I tried to think back to the conversations I'd had with my mother. Somehow, they had all been about a different kind of birth. I would be there, holding her hand, stroking her face. The baby would emerge, clean and pink, and I would be there to wrap it and care for it. This picture looked nothing like the ones I'd imagined, but at least I could do that much.

I laid the little body down on the floor while I fetched one of the less-filthy cloths. It startled, throwing its arms and legs wide, and I realised it was a boy. I wrapped the length of fabric around the tiny form, then held it to me again. It shuddered a little, and then went still. Good. It probably needed to sleep. Ignoring the frantic motions of the women at the bedside, I clambered onto my parents' bed, dragging my bundle with me. I settled myself right in the centre of the bed, curled around the body of my brother like a chick in the egg, wrapped around its yolk sac. We could sleep together.

That was where Father found us. I woke suddenly as he tried to draw the small bundle from my arms. Shrieking, I fought him off. I wasn't really awake yet – just completely conscious that I had to protect my brother. From everyone. He hit me, two flat-handed blows across the face.

I fell back again, into the stiffened, filthy, blood-reeking sheets. He reached again to take the baby and I wriggled away, backing into the corner of the room, still holding my precious burden. Looking back now, my behaviour seems strange, even mad. What reason had I to be afraid of my own father? But I think now that I knew, already knew all that was to come.

He came forward again, more gently, and reached for me, stopping again as I shrank back. 'Give it to me, Tiris. I need to bury it.'

'No, no. I promised Mama I'd look after him.'

'And you did, girl. You did just as you were asked. But it's time to let go now.'

'He needs me.'

'He's dead, Tiris. There's nothing more you can do.'

'No. Father, no!'

I bent to the little bundle of rags I cradled and pulled the cloth back from his face. It was true. The wizened face was still and blue. There was no sound of breath, no movement or warmth. I held him close to me and rocked, crooning. He couldn't be dead. I'd promised Mama I'd take care of him. I looked up at Father.

'Mama?'

A terrible expression crossed his face, and he turned away, wrapping his hands around himself and gripping his own arms fiercely. 'Jana.' The name was forced from him. He took great gulps of air, getting himself under control again, before turning back to me. He held out one hand. The arm was stiff, but his fingers were shaking.

'Give him to me,'

I took a step towards him, and then another. And then he was lifting the burden from me, taking it to himself, but wrapping his other arm around me and pulling me close to him as the tears burst from my eyes.

Thank you to everyone who contributed to this book, giving of their time and energy so freely. Thank you again to the people who have bought it, the difference you have made to the Romanian rescuers and the animals they fight daily to save is immeasurable.